AGE OF MOBILE DATA

THE WIRELESS JOURNEY TO ALL DATA 4G NETWORKS

Majeed Ahmad

SMARTPHONE CHRONICLE

This publication is designed to provide accurate and authoritative information in regard to the subject matter covered. It is sold with the understanding that the publisher is not engaged in rendering professional services. The advice and strategies contained herein may not be suitable for your situation. You should consult with a professional where appropriate. Neither the publisher nor author shall be liable for any loss of profit or any other commercial damages, including but not limited to special, incidental, consequential, or other damages.

ISBN 10: 1494749114
ISBN 13: 978-1494749118
Library of Congress Control Number: 2014902067
CreateSpace Independent Publishing Platform
North Charleston, South Carolina

Dedicated to Alcatel—my first employer

CONTENTS

PROLOGUE

"A phone getting video can only get so much data. If you had 10 Mbit/s, what are you going to do with it?"

—Allen Nogee, principal analyst, In-Stat, in a
2010 interview with *Ars Technica*

In June 2010, AT&T delivered the new smartphone economy a wake-up call when it decided to scrap unlimited data plans for its customers. When the iPhone launched in 2007, AT&T charged US$20 a month for unlimited data usage. Now AT&T subscribers would no longer have the option to pay a flat fee for unlimited data, which they had since the birth of iPhone-driven smartphone economy. AT&T's abrupt reversal to metered data usage prompted a backlash from bloggers and consumers alike. AT&T, on the other hand, faced a dreadful dilemma. The second-largest U.S. wireless company had been battling network congestion as it tried to manage a soaring demand unleashed by the data-hungry devices like the iPhone.

In the mid-2000's, U.S. wireless operators like AT&T and Verizon spent a fortune rolling out third generation (3G) networks. If you built it, everyone assumed, they would come. But no one came and their costly 3G networks spent a few years being heavily underused. Mobile phones were little devices that had the WAP-based applications that were mostly lousy and failed to gain any traction. Then, the iPhone came to the AT&T's network in 2007, and the carrier enticed subscribers by offering them unlimited access to the mobile Internet. The iPhone took off, Android quickly followed the smartphone revolution, and the mobile industry changed forever. Now, in a strange about-face, AT&T executives began to criticize smartphone users as data hogs.

The industry watchers predicted that bandwidth demands on mobile phone networks would grow exponentially as more people got smartphones and as they adopted smartphone-like devices such as the iPad, which were billed as suited for a host of bandwidth-intensive applications like streaming video. Until now, AT&T had largely been able to manage that growth by making billions of dollars of network improvements across the United States. However, several times during 2009, AT&T had been reportedly hit by network outages in cities like San Francisco and New York, places with high concentrations of people using iPhones and other smartphone devices. The connectivity and speed issues were plaguing AT&T's iPhone user base, and consequently, much more bandwidth was needed.

Another case study on the critical importance of wireless networks in the smartphone age came from Google's unveiling of the Nexus One handset in January 2009; Google attempted to separate the phone from its competitors by calling it a super-phone. But soon after the launch, users began complaining about spotty data network reception and non-existent customer services, which made the user experience disappointingly mediocre. The Nexus One debacle was a testament that hand-helds were no smarter than the systems built to operate them. The overwhelmed AT&T network episode further made the case that smartphones could be data hogs and that wireless networks needed to carefully calibrate data usage in order to survive the stress and strain on the overall network performance.

Since the arrival of the iPhone, industry experts had seen incredible strides in mobile hardware and software, and it was getting to the point where they were hesitating to call these microcomputers phones. Smartphone capabilities went far beyond what mobile users would expect from simple voice telephony. As to the smartphone's existence before the iPhone, industry experts pointed to the fact that the network resources to cater for something like a BlackBerry were radically different from and much less than those needed for the iPhone. The BlackBerry mainly catered to e-mail where the traffic was compressed, and it was only one session per user. Moreover, BlackBerry devices were very operator-friendly. The iPhone, on the other hand, was a computing platform on which the user could run applications like Google Maps, which could open up as many as three hundred sessions through the Internet.

The media attention in the mobile phone arena had long been focused on the battle between super smartphones. However, there was a parallel campaign underway among wireless carriers to roll out new, faster data networks to link these sophisticated handheld computers to the Internet at greater speeds and to increase the capacity to handle all the data their owners were downloading. The goal was to overcome capacity limitations and make wireless Internet access on the street as fast as the access people got in homes and offices.

But would there be sufficient network bandwidth to support the dramatic increase in mobile data usage? Mobile phone operators were evidently having difficulties in keeping up with data traffic demand amid a mindboggling trend: data traffic had exceeded voice traffic in the post-iPhone era. At this juncture, it was also predicted that within a few years, the mobile Internet would surpass the cellular phone system as a far better communications network. The futurists said that voice connectivity in the iPhone-like devices could subsequently serve the same function as the VHS slot found in many DVD players: legacy support.

In fact, even in the early stages, the iPhone had started causing the troubling problems of dropped calls and digital brown-outs. Smartphones drove data traffic over mobile networks to new levels, thereby requiring new technologies to keep up with the frenetic demand. The transition had also caused incredibly fast changes in wireless operators' networks and business models. They found themselves in the data business, but not the way they planned to be in the data business. They had in fact planned for Internet Protocol (IP) networks to deal with data but not on the scale they were experiencing in the post-iPhone settings.Now, apart from the ongoing evolution of the cellular standards to higher data rates and efficiency, there was hope that Wi-Fi would play an important role in helping to offload data traffic from overworked cellular networks.

AT&T had set the bar for smartphones and proved a handset could conceive data services on wireless platforms. By doing so, it created the same kind of game-changing event that the iPhone had accomplished in terms of creating a new user demand on the device front. Prior to the emergence of smartphones, wireless operator's loyalty was tied more to the network coverage. In the early days of cellular, there wasn't much difference between most voice-only handsets. There were the size and fashion considerations, or more interest in devices that offered a wider range of compatible accessories. But phones were just phones. Then came the smartphone, and with it came more device differentiations and a greater range of handset capabilities.

The iPhone's ascendance to fame had one thing written all over it: all services of the network are represented by the phone. So AT&T's iPhone liaison forced competitors such as Verizon to accept the idea that the handset was an instrument of network service, not a mere accessory for fulfilling of it. Wireless carriers like Verizon were now willing to integrate the handset into their service offerings rather than simply using it as a mechanism for getting the consumer onto the wireless network. The smartphone represented a monumental shift for the wireless industry, and with it, the handset had transformed from being a carrier- or vendor-controlled device to a computing platform.

Wireless carriers were used to build their own agenda into cell phone designs, but Apple's union with AT&T had changed that model. The iPhone cracked open the carrier-centric structure of the wireless industry and unlocked a host of benefits for consumers, developers, manufacturers, and for carriers themselves. For wireless operators, as the number of radios grew, networks began to matter a lot more than before. Wireless carriers in the United States, who saw AT&T eating into their customer base, started scrambling to find a competitive device, and they appeared willing to give up some authority to get it. The AT&T episode had shown that having good handset hardware and software mattered, and having good networks mattered, too.

After the iPhone ascent and the subsequent AT&T's data snag, the industry was unanimous in its verdict: it's the network.

The next few years were going to be crucial as the mobile industry negotiated this seismic shift from voice to mobile data and from the PC-centric to the mobile-centric Internet. Not every wireless operator, infrastructure supplier, and device maker was going to make it. Smartphone's disruptive era had already witnessed the fall of Nokia and the dissolution of Motorola on the device front and the collapse of Nortel Networks in the infrastructure domain. Next, wireless operators were likely to struggle to understand their emerging role in the mobile broadband age. Their mobile data revenues were set to pass mobile voice revenues by the end of 2013. So mobile phone operators would find themselves facing a fundamentally different kind of business. They were going to look more like Internet service providers (ISPs) than phone companies.

1  THE PIONEER ERA

"The implications of mobile data traffic doubling every year are profound."

—John Donovan, AT&T's senior executive vice president of technology and network operations in a 2012 post on the company's Innovation Space blog

Wireless got into the networking game once technologists became confident that data could travel across the airwaves. Still, the beginning of wireless data was accidental as well as circumstantial. Wireless data chronicles reveal that though the concept had long been the staple of science fiction stories, its genesis could actually be traced to the 1970 experiments of Norman Abramson at the University of Hawaii, when he developed a 4.8 Kbit/s packet-radio network. Aloha, meaning hello in Hawaiian, connected an IBM 360 mainframe in the main campus on the island of Oahu to card readers and terminals dispersed among different islands and ships at sea. Eventually, Abramson's work became the foundation for packet radio as well as Ethernet-based local area network (LAN) systems.

The next act in the history of mobile data came in 1979 when scientists at the Advanced Research Projects Agency (ARPA) started looking for variable transmission venues to confirm the viability of what would later become the Internet. The Internet's mentor body funded the "Packet Radio Network" project in which experiments were carried out by establishing communication links between mobile vans. The outcome was a multiple-hop wireless network with an extremely low channel frequency and bulky terminals. These were the early days for the notion of wireless data, which would become a reality only after about two decades with improvements in bandwidth, processing power, miniaturization, and power consumption.

During this period, corporate America got a starter in mobile data with systems meant for two-way messaging services for fleet delivery. The initial impetus broadly came from transport, security, and field service sectors, which had traditionally been using dispatch systems based on land mobile radio (LMR) technology. Their mobile workers, who wanted corporate access while away from the office, were keen to use wireless data services. In the 1970s, for instance, FedEx built a U.S.-wide wireless data network to keep track of its packages using a proprietary radio technology. During this period, it became clear that packet radio was highly suitable for the applications characterized by relatively short bursts of data, such as messaging, point-of-sale (POS) transactions, database queries and fleet dispatch.

However, despite forecasts suggesting a massive swing toward wireless data, the larger take-off was just not happening. That's because historically mobile communications at large had focused on handling simple telephony services. The first-generation cellular systems were designed purely for voice communications, so while mobile phone usage grew at exponential rates, wireless data remained in low profile. Several factors also hampered the use of mobile data applications in the public arena. Low data rates, expensive airtime, and unfriendly services that were difficult to configure and run were the major constraints. Another important factor was the terminal evolution.

However, though wireless data market remained in doldrums, there were some prominent efforts to carve out important niches in this area. Advanced Radio Data Information Service (ARDIS) was the first major packet data-messaging system created in 1983 as a private network for fifteen thousand IBM service technicians in the United States. Motorola had built the technology as DataTac and sold it to IBM so that Big Blue's customer service teams could diagnose and repair IBM mainframe computers using Motorola's KDT mobile terminals. ARDIS comprised of radio base stations covering fifteen to twenty miles, network controllers and network control centers and supported 19.2 Kbit/s data rate in 25 kHz channels. It eventually became a public mobile data service as a joint venture between IBM and Motorola.

IBM later sold its interests to Motorola in 1994, and ARDIS became a subsidiary of Motorola. Earlier in 1989, Hutchison Telecom of Hong Kong had launched an ARDIS-based mobile data service in a joint venture with Motorola. However, after failing to get subscribers, in 1994, Hutchison sold its 70 percent stakes to Motorola, who eventually formed a subsidiary company Motorola Air Communications that launched wireless data service under the Max brand name next year.

Meanwhile, recognizing the need for two-way wireless data communications, engineers at Televerket—which later became Telia—started work in collaboration with Ericsson. It's worthwhile to mention that the Swedish telecom gearmaker, like neighboring Nokia, had flirted with the computer business for quite a while during the 1980s. Eventually, Ericsson and Televerket Radio conceived a mobile data technology as a private mobile alarm system for field personnel. The two companies built a low-speed data network at 1.2 Kbit/s with a text-based voice dispatch overlay. Mobitex used hierarchical structure and was the first mobile data technology to offer seamless roaming and battery-saving features. The mobile data network put a great emphasis on safety and reliability amid its potential use by military, police, firefighters and ambulance services.

Commercial Mobitex operation started in Sweden in 1986, and the technology was significantly enhanced four years later for use in the United States, Europe, and Australia. From 1988 onward, the development of Mobitex took place under the umbrella of Eritel, a joint-venture between Ericsson and Televerket; Eritel became an Ericsson subsidiary later on. Meanwhile, in 1993, the Swedish government-owned Televerket became Telia AB as a result of telecommunication deregulation. Telia, in turn, became part of TeliaSonera later on.

Mobitex terminals were typically standard notebook PCs equipped with a radio modem, or they were dedicated mobile terminals. The user interface was packet-based, data-only system incorporating cellular architecture, multichannel frequency reuse and store-and-forward capability at data rates of up to 8 Kbit/s. It became a de facto standard for packet-switched mobile data networks after RAM Mobile Data—a partnership between RAM Broadcasting and U.S. telecom service provider BellSouth—introduced a Mobitex-based service in the United States in 1991. In the mid-1990s, Mobitex gained popularity by providing two-way paging network services. The early BlackBerry e-mail devices communicated using this text-only network; Mobitex also provided refuge to the much-hyped Palm VII launch in 1999.

Ironically, while Mobitex had been exported to the United States, American ARDIS technology was being deployed in Europe. Both Mobitex and ARDIS were public mobile data services based on proprietary technologies. They were built around the principle of specialized mobile radio, and they used portable radio terminals that were expensive and heavy. But their major drawback was low-data throughput that typically ranged from 2.4 Kbit/s to 4.8 Kbit/s. Although later upgraded to 19.2 Kbit/s, data throughput practically remained below 8 Kbit/s due to overhead related to radio channel protocol and error-correction procedures.

THE TERMINAL SIDE

GRiD Systems, a small computer outfit on the east of the San Francisco Bay, was a pioneer in mobile computing, and many of the technologies present in notebooks and tablet PCs wouldn't exist were it not for GRiD. Jeff Hawkins was considered the main architect of GRiD's pen-based computing program. The success of his product designs gave Hawkins a modest amount of fame as a pioneer of the fledging pen-computer industry. A self-assured and brilliant product designer, he firmly believed that the future of personal computing was in portable electronic devices. In 1991, Hawkins, like so many technology entrepreneurs before him, was in the grip of an idea for a new type of computer. To chase that dream, Hawkins left GRiD with a license for software he needed and started Palm Computing on January 2, 1992.

The handheld computer market was doomed after Apple introduced its infamous Newton, but Hawkins kept going with the help of Donna Dubinsky, a Harvard MBA with an impressive Silicon Valley track record, and marketing whiz Ed Colligan. After a two-year design effort, a simple, no-frills compact device hit the market in February 1996 under a larger corporate umbrella of U.S. Robotics. Palm Computing had come perilously close to running out of cash during these years, forcing the troika to sell their company to modem king U.S. Robotics, which, in turn, was purchased by network hardware maker 3Com. Palm Pilot became one of the fastest-selling high-tech toys of the decade. The elegant little computer that Hawkins and his team of idealists brought to life against all odds became an American icon. One million Palm Pilots were sold in the first eighteen months.

The advent of Palm seemed like such a portentous leap into the future, but the lack of some kind of interactivity could dwarf its widescale implementation, or so thought many industry observers. The personal digital assistant (PDA), once a glorified address book, was now increasingly seen as a steppingstone in the convergence of mobile platforms. The conventional wisdom had it that wireless—providing the ability to surf the web or check e-mails from an untethered handheld or cell phone—would be the biggest thing since the dawn of Internet itself. So industry analysts were almost unanimous in their belief that a handheld computer wouldn't succeed until it included, at the very least, fax and e-mail functions. They questioned the Pilot's lack of wireless capability and PCMCIA expansion card slot.

At that time, during the mid-1990s, Motorola, Nokia, and Sony were developing communicators while IBM and BellSouth were collaborating on a cellular-palmtop hybrid, which would eventually become the first smartphone launched at the commercial scale: Simon. Jeff Hawkins, on the other hand, had set his eyes on creating the ultimate organizer and didn't want to dilute its effectiveness with communications features. However, the disconnected handheld models were mostly perceived as fancy organizers. So, in the end, the future of the PDA merely came down to a simple choice: connected or not!

According to Hawkins, there was a huge market out there if only there was the right kind of portable electronics product. People wanted a great mobile phone, a great pager, and a great organizer, he argued. Hawkins said that designers of wireless devices would subsequently grapple with many unknown factors. The challenges included not only choosing the right wireless network, radio, and battery but also determining exactly what consumers would want in the way of features. Did they want e-mail or mobile web or access to corporate networks? All these were pieces in the puzzle, all were interconnected, and all were moving targets.

Back in the mid-1990s, Hawkins felt certain that all handheld computers would one day have wireless functions, but that day was a long way off. The basic problem, as he saw it, was the shape of wireless networks and that the available network technologies were too immature for satisfying wireless palmtop. Wireless circuitry would impose a dramatic battery drain, would make the device far bulkier, and would deliver the Internet at snail-like speeds, which users would find unacceptable. Hawkins wanted to wait until the technologies had improved. However, U.S. Robotics executives started pushing him to develop a wireless version, one that would send and receive information without the need for a phone line and a modem. Hawkins figured out it would take two years to come up with a wireless Palm Pilot.

In the end, it wound up taking three years, finally seeing the light of the day in May 1999, bearing the name Palm VII. The idea about Palm VII was to build a two-way radio, which, riding the BellSouth data network via a flip-up antenna, would allow users to tap into the Internet and send and receive e-mails without a modem and phone line. The vehicle of Palm Pilot's launch on airwaves was the decade-old RAM Mobile Data network, which had now acquired the name BellSouth Mobile Data. Despite noble efforts of RAM Mobile Data, which built the wireless data network in the early 1990s, users didn't flock to the service. However, once BellSouth scooped up the company in 1998 and backed it with marketing and branding, the network quickly filled up.

BellSouth—one of the last standard-bearers of Graham Bell—had been evangelizing the embryonic mobile date industry for quite some time; it was also the first telephone company to set up a subsidiary for data services. Now, the Baby Bell was offering mobile data services to 90 percent of the urban business population in its coverage territory in the southeastern United States through a network based on Ericsson's Mobitex technology. BellSouth wireless data network provided crucial services to the big U.S. companies to enable them stay connected with their workforce in the field. Naturally, Palm's new owner 3Com turned to BellSouth for providing communications services on its palmtop organizers. BellSouth, on the other hand, needed the small form factor for devices operating on its data network. That made up the foundation of this venture.

Taking the Palm Pilot form factor and its basic organizer features, the two companies envisioned tapping into the power of the web to bring the world's first successful Internet appliance. Hawkins, then at 3Com's Palm Computing division, sat with the president of BellSouth wireless data unit to hash out details of the new-born Palm.net. In the summer of 1999, using web clipping format, Palm VII handheld enabled users to check stock quotes and weather information and to buy tickets online through specific websites. Instead of trying to display a complete, downloaded web page on the tiny screen, the Palm VII would be preloaded with mini web pages, complete with graphics, blanks, and pop-up menus. Data from the web would appear in the appropriate blanks: stock prices, news articles, movie schedules, sports scores, phone book information, and so on.

Because only tiny snippets of text would be transferred, each web lookup would take only a few seconds. Within a year of Palm VII launch, the customer base of BellSouth grew from 200,000 users to 570,000. The Baby Bell added three hundred base stations to the network and renamed the network as Cingular Interactive. However, though the long-awaited wireless data capability brought forth a new era of portability, serious technical and market hurdles still persisted. Palm VII was radically different from the handheld maker's other products; not only in having wireless features but also in its higher price—US$599. So despite initially revitalizing the BellSouth's wireless data network, it never became a hit like Palm III or Palm V.

Computer scientists had been predicting the advent of such information appliances for decades. And now Palm, which had single-handedly generated the PDA craze and had succeeded where many had failed before, was leading a drive into the brave new wireless world. However, in retrospect, Hawkins had been right in rejecting the notion of adding superfluous new features that only a selected few would use. Palm VII was eventually regarded as an early entrant in the nascent world of mobile data services. The machine was years ahead of its time. Wireless mobile computing, however, would remain a hot button in the industry for years to come.

PDA–PHONE RENDEZVOUS

Just when the PDA started meaning a Palm Pilot, there came a turning point in the short history of handheld computers. Although Palm had become a flagship product of 3Com, the parent company was known as a networking powerhouse, and its limited vision for handheld computers was frustrating for the Palm founders. In 1998, after failing to convince 3Com to spin off the Palm unit and to invest more in the development of the product, Hawkins and Dubinsky left 3Com to start their own handheld-computing company, Handspring Inc. Ed Colligan would soon join ranks with his old comrades.

Shortly afterward, 3Com's offshoot Handspring announced a new product based on Palm operating system. The trio who had brought the world the Palm Pilot struck again, bringing a faster, cheaper, and far more versatile handheld computer within a period of one year after founding Handspring. The new gadget—named Visor—introduced the innovative plug-and-play capability in handheld computers to add paging, audio, and camera modules. Communications met computing met consumer electronics!

Visor's biggest asset—its easy-to-use expansion slot called the Springboard—could virtually turn the device into any consumer or communications appliance. The savvy Palm clone with an expansion slot could transform the gadget into anything from a GPS receiver to an MP3 player. After sliding the module into its slot, the module automatically installed its software and began running no matter what the Visor was doing at that time. Once a user was done with the module, he or she could take it out; the program uninstalled itself instantly and disappeared. In fact, the advent of Visor had marked the birth of the smartphone all over again, and once more, the prodigy came from the computing side. The expandable PDA gave handheld devices a new direction, making Palm handheld look like a pedestrian.

Visor was absolutely stunning; it became a Wall Street star overnight. The upstart founded by Palm alumni had mapped out an effective media blitz. Now the Palm fans were anxiously waiting for this magic device, but what happened next could serve as a textbook example for any startup company. Visor, which suddenly emerged on the commercial scene, ended up in a severe inventory crisis. A brisk web sale followed the product launch, and then, Handspring crumbled under pressure from component shortage and hardware problems. Product glitches and delivery delays led to a logistic nightmare; people were looking for gadget all over but could not find it for many months to come. Visor became a victim of its own success.

However, once the dust settled after Visor's pop icon standing and logistic debacle, it turned out that its biggest asset—easy-to-use expansion slot—could also become a liability. Two inches long and half an inch deep slot used so much space that it made users wonder why they had to carry a bag full of Springboard stuff. Consequently, Handspring abandoned the Visor line of organizers to focus on developing mobile phone combined with a data gadget. Though Visor was a modest business success, the notion behind the realization of Visor carried far more revolutionary implications. Soon a stream of elegant concepts began to appear in the marketplace, evangelizing what a PDA could do as a portable electronic device.

It'd been more than a decade since the three-person firm called Palm Computing had opened for business, but the handheld industry was still in its infancy. Hawkins saw the handheld computer industry as embryonic; he would quote the famous analogy "It's like 1982 of the PC world." With all the attention on wireless-ready PDA, it was becoming hard to remember that most PDAs in use didn't have a wireless connection of any kind, and a good number of their owners probably didn't want one. A spate of consumer surveys indicated that wireless wasn't necessarily everything when it came to PDAs, despite what market analysts tended to say in unison.

Wireless Internet had been touted as the next big thing since the late 1990s. The technology gurus argued that once the wireless Internet began to take off, giving users access to the web through portable computers would be a no-brainer. That could put the PDA at the heart of always-on wireless nirvana, changing the landscape of communications as well as of computing for many years to come. That's one reason why "always-on" was something of an object of great optimism to PDA zealots. But was the PDA the ideal platform for web surfing? The first problem was limited coverage. Although companies such as BellSouth provided Internet access to handheld devices like Palm, having a built-in wireless modem, network coverage was spotty at best.

While Palms worked well in major metropolitan areas of the United States, they had difficulty connecting beyond those boundaries. Another problem with wireless data networks was the slow rate at which they delivered the web pages. These networks were mostly working at a speed of 9.6 Kbit/s, which was fine for plain text but was too slow for ordinary web pages with any kind of graphics. There was a possibility of a wireless setup offering higher data rates of up to 14.4 Kbit/s, but that required the use of a modem and cell phone and, hence, wires to establish connections. Some industry circles closer to the wireless sector hoped that GPRS would also complement the PDA. But the new data-enabled wireless networks like GPRS were taking shape at a slower pace than makers of handheld computing devices would have expected.

Soon after the inception of Symbian in 1998, and conse-quently the "smartphone" splash, handheld designers began their DNA splicing experiments will cellular phones. The most exciting competition in personal technology was the race to design the best communicator, a new kind of handheld device that combined a wireless phone and modem, a digital orga-nizer, and an e-mail and web terminal. These smartphones were primarily light voice terminals that got their smarts from the ability to display calendars, send and receive e-mails, and play music files. Conversely, a slight alteration came in the form of PDA phones: handheld computers that were mainly intended for wireless data communications, but they also doubled as phones. These devices often had shiny screens, lots of tiny buttons and, usually, a stylus. They all promised some sort of Internet on the move, e-mail, and so on. In the hindsight, however, they didn't get a single one of these func-tions to work flawlessly.

Still, smartphone shipments surged 400 percent in the first quarter of 2003. Slowly and steadily, the pieces of the smart-phone puzzle were falling in place. Then in 2007 came the defin-ing moment in the PDA's metamorphosis into the smartphone. Apple took its largely unfinished business that it had started with Newton and effectively turned it into a PDA which could make calls and most importantly had excellent web-browsing ability. The form factor of the iPhone did strike some resemblance with the all-screen look of the Newton MessagePad. Fourteen years after Apple had released the Newton—a handheld device with handwriting recognition, desktop syncing, and an embrace of third-party applications—the Cupertino, California–based com-pany was proudly showing its descendant hailed by the industry as a revolutionary and magical product.

The PDA had quietly emerged into a powerful and rich tool for personal digital management. Then the rude awakening came when the industry witnessed portable computer pioneers like Handspring and consumer electronics bellwethers such as Sony giving up PDA product lineups one by one. For some, it was about time to declare the demise of the handheld computer or the PDA, which many people in IT industry thought would become ubiquitous someday. "PDA is dead," proclaimed Symbian chief David Levin in fall 2003. The PDA—the portable monument of the late twentieth century and early twenty-first century vision of ubiquitous computing—was indeed folding into the annals of technology history.

In the final analysis, it was now beyond any doubt that the world's most popular electronic gadget was the mobile phone. The old and new mobile phone establishments were now betting that enough of the things that people wanted from the Internet could work without a personal computer's big screen. Despite the smaller display of cellular handsets, users were still able to send and receive e-mails, perform e-commerce transactions, and get real-time updates on such things as travel, weather, news, and sporting events. They claimed that by combining smartphones with the wireless Internet, computing might achieve its apotheosis: simple, reliable, ubiquitous, and pervasive.

THE RICOCHET SAGA

Another classical case study on the premise that the future of mobile data belonged to cellular mainstream came from the

Ricochet saga. In 1995, Metricom Inc., in a spirit of a true pioneer, launched its road warrior service, embracing a plan to build a data-only mobile network covering dense, metropolitan areas of the United States. The San Jose, California–based company deployed radio antennas on the top of poles and traffic lights across the entire city to create the so-called microcells, small geographic areas that allowed its Ricochet network to offer widescale coverage. These radio base stations passed signals to wired access points, typically placed on building rooftops, in turn, connected to the core network through T1 leased lines. Ricochet users plugged a US$99 custom modem into their laptops to communicate with pole-top base stations, the access points on every sixth or eighth street lamp in major cities.

The wireless network gave users online access at more than twice the speed of standard dial-up telephone modems, and worked from the back of taxicabs, in hotel lobbies, and almost every other urban nook-and-cranny. Mobile users were offered laptop connectivity at a flat rate of US$40 per month for a speed of 64 Kbit/s and US$70 per month for 128 Kbit/s. The popularity of the Ricochet network stemmed from its speed and reliability. Metricom wanted to provide enough coverage and capacity so that its subscribers could move around at 70 miles per hour in cars and still send and receive e-mails. The San Jose–based firm was targeting mobile business professionals as its primary users. The mobile data pioneer went through a great hardship and spent US$1.1 billion of investment pool to build a competent mobile-data network at a furious pace.

Metricom was founded in 1985 to develop technology for utilities to check meters remotely. Ten years later, it launched the Ricochet wireless data service that initially operated at

28.8 Kbit/s. While moving up on the speed ladder, the company eventually got caught up in the great building binge that overwhelmed the telecommunications industry in the late 1990s. Its managers boasted that this provider of high-speed wireless access to the Internet would become the Sprint of the mobile data world. The dream was shattered in the summer of 2001 when Metricom shut down its network, putting an end to one of the most visible efforts to bring mobile Internet access to the masses. Over 51,000 subscribers across a seventeen-city network, approximately US$1 billion debt and Chapter 11 bankruptcy filing—that's how far the maverick Metricom would go.

The company remained optimistic right up to the end that it could leverage its unique position as the first wireless-networking service provider to the mobile road warriors. People had a real passion for the product. So what killed Metricom? For a start, it was inconvenient to lug a 3-7 lb laptop around to do things that mobile users should be able to do over a PDA or cellphone. The strength of mobility was in its ability to communicate while moving, but in Ricochet-like service models, it was difficult to differentiate whether a user was moving or stationary. In reality, Metricom's primary consumers ended up sitting in their homes using the Ricochet service as a fixed-wireless Internet access medium. Furthermore, the large wireless modem attached to the laptop was awkward and gave Ricochet the image of yesterday's wireless technology with today's computing. Apart from the mobile modem, Aircard, the US$99 "brick" connected to a laptop, there was an antenna sticking out of laptop, which often made fellow business travelers curious.

Metricom didn't have the proper audience targeted for its service, or the right product available for the type of audience it was targeting. One of the logical conclusions from the Metricom saga was that when it comes to mobility, people prefer a small form factor. That happened earlier in the voice-telephony arena when the wireless industry dumped the car phones and hand-carrying portable phones for handheld phones. It was apparent by now that mobile Internet could become popular through more portable form factors—like mobile phone—and that Ricochet would become forgotten victim of the concept it tried to promote. Ricochet was better than any other type of mobile data service on the market; wireless gadgets like the Blackberry pager and the Palm VII handheld computer provided only limited access to the Internet. However, most people didn't necessarily want full Internet access on the go, so the Blackberry device—primarily used for e-mail—caught on like wildfire.

It's also worthwhile to note that after establishing itself in high-tech centers like San Francisco, Metricom expanded fast across the United States only at a time when the rest of the technology market was heading south. It took ten long years for Metricom to develop its mobile data service, and by the time it was up and running, the economic downturn of the early 2000s had hit dotcoms and telecommunications companies the hardest. Metricom had one foot in each sector. Industry analysts also blamed Metricom's zigzag marketing strategy for not making the benefits known to the marketplace. They said, "People don't buy technology; they buy what technology does for them." The Metricom technology was first-rate, so it was tempting to blame the business plan or the marketing strategy, or both.

Ricochet's far-better-than-narrowband mobile capability would still remain a high-water mark in the Internet connectivity arena. Unlike cellular data rates, often having a lot more sophistry than speed, Ricochet's advertised 128 Kbit/s speed was an atypically honest number; users usually got that rate and sometimes a lot more, as much as 180 Kbit/s. However, despite Ricochet's strengths, the network never became popular beyond a niche audience. Costing as much as US$75 a month, it was too pricey for all but serious Internet junkies. Many experts agreed that Ricochet service filled a gap, but in this case, the first-mover advantage proved only a myth. Now, while the Ricochet was gone, mobile users would have to wait for 3G services and even 3G network could come at lower speeds and higher prices. Such services would likely charge per minute or per packet, a far cry from Ricochet's unlimited access.

Ricochet was appreciated after its demise. Metricom's rapid rollout highlighted the potential demand for the service. The rave customer reviews for Ricochet service were a testimonial to the quality and untapped potential of the mobile data technology. Though its failure to build a national footprint cost the company everything it had, the Silicon Valley firm had indeed paved the way for other companies to advance mobile data services. Another great idea that was ahead of its time! What Metricom offered was a glimpse of the future.

Motorola's KDT 480 was one of the first popular mobile data terminals operating on the ARDIS system. Motorola has often celebrated its pioneering role in walkie-talkies, color television and cellular communications, but the Schaumburg, Illinois–based consumer electronics giant has also been a major innovator in the mobile data realm. It co-developed the DataTac mobile data technology along with IBM which eventually became the world's first public mobile data network: ARDIS.

Photo credit: IPriori, Inc.

Ericsson's Åke Johansson is known as Mr. Mobitex for his lead role in the development of the European public mobile data network. Ericsson launched Mobitex network back in 1986 in collaboration with Televerket, the Swedish government-owned telecom service provider which later became Telia AB as a result of telecom deregulation of the 1990s.

Photo courtesy of Ericsson

Handspring's Visor PDA—though a modest business success—eventually became a precursor to the smartphone. Visor's expansion slot could virtually turn the device into any consumer electronics or communication appliance.

Photo: *Pen Computing*

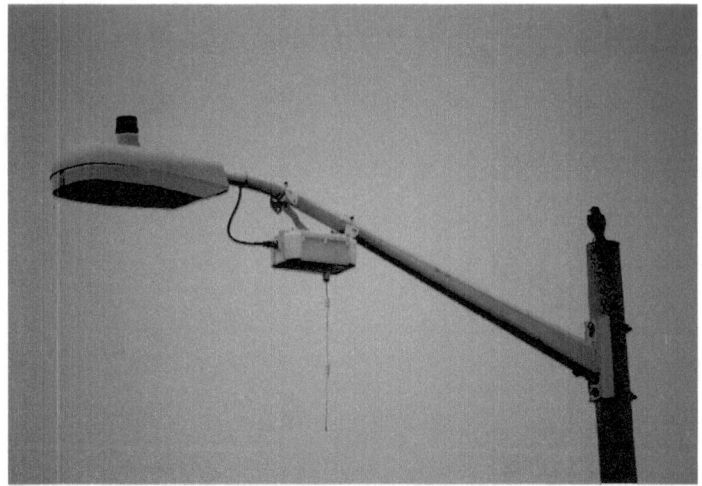

Metricom deployed radio antennas on poles and traffic lights across the entire city to create micro-cells for its Ricochet mobile data network. Ricochet users plugged a custom modem into their laptops to communicate with the pole-top radio base stations.

Photo credit: Flickr user Constantine Hannaher

2  CELLULAR TWILIGHT

"This is more of a step toward full 3G."

—Brenda Raney, spokeswoman for Verizon
Wireless on 2.5G wireless networks

For a start, though dial-up modems could work on mobile phone lines, major cellular operators in the United States felt the need of a service specifically designed for data applications. Their collaboration with IBM resulted in the Cellular Digital Packet Data (CDPD) system in 1992. A packet data overlay to the existing analog cellular infrastructures such as AMPS, it used idle voice channels to send short data messages by hopping among available frequencies. The CDPD spec was the first open mobile data standard against proprietary ARDIS and Mobitex systems and thus brought a new data communication model. It also introduced the IP element into mobile communications for the first time.

The CDPD network was suitable for applications based on small bursts of data, such as e-mail, database queries, and credit card authorization. Its support for IP also went to its advantage at the time of the Internet take-off. Although the first CDPD specification was released in July 1993, initial rollouts were not complete until the mid-1990s. To access the data, the salespeople were given laptops and PC Card modems from Sierra Wireless Inc. that could use both wireline and wireless CDPD connections.

Sierra Wireless was founded in 1993 by a team of engineers who were instrumental in defining the CDPD standard while working at MPR Teltech, the Burnaby, British Columbia–based company which had developed and marketed mobile data products for over ten years. American wireless pioneer McCaw Cellular was another leading supporter of the mobile data protocol. Ameritech, AT&T Wireless, and GTE were also among the first to deploy CDPD in the United States. Also, using CDPD technology in 1994, Carnegie Mellon University set up one of the largest wireless data networks—Wireless Andrew.

The CDPD system used a forward error correction scheme to combat the interference and fading of cellular channels, so the impact of voice traffic on CDPD was supposed to be negligible. On the downside, however, CDPD required a modem with a mobile terminal for the user and an upgrade at the radio base station for the operator. Notebook and PDA users could run data applications at 19.2 Kbit/s using a combination of a PC Card and a wireless modem. But the actual throughput was reduced to 10 Kbit/s to 13 Kbit/s due to system overhead. Consequently, most of the mobile phone companies became reluctant to deploy it, and despite some market penetration during the mid-1990s, CDPD ended up as an underused interim solution.

Mobile data was repeatedly predicted a boom market but applications such as ARDIS, CDPD, and Mobitex only served small niches in vertical markets. Many products had come and gone in their quest of exploiting the wireless data promise. There were multiple devices, multiple approaches to build networks, and multiple ways of delivering and aggregating content over mobile data systems. At one stage, it seemed as if there was no genuine need for wireless data except niche applications such as vehicle dispatch. The opponents said that mobile data was a drag and that mobile phone users didn't want much data; they just wanted tailored information in the form of well-thought-out applications.

The idea had long been a disappointing stepchild to the industry with often-stated "year of the mobile data" slogan perpetually coming in the following year. Although mobile data systems like CDPD and Mobitex had fulfilled their role in nurturing the natural technology advancement, the market still needed a breakthrough, a killer application of some sort, to go any further from here. Only mass-market appeal could save the promise of this potentially great idea. Then, the humble text message emerged as a turning point, providing the much-needed breakthrough from a corridor nobody in the wireless industry was originally looking at. Mobile data, which had long been a dream of technologists, got its first practical manifestation from a source no one had envisioned through all these years.

GSM AT CROSSROADS

Mobile data was screaming for applications as it needed some kind of kick-start, which short message service (SMS) would subsequently provide. On one hand, SMS caused the demise of paging, and on the other hand, it laid the groundwork for a new era in mobile data applications. With text messaging, wireless data landed in the masses for the first time, although there was nothing smart about it. Before SMS, originally built to exchange small text messages across GSM networks, sending data over cellular platforms was never an easy proposition. Although cellular systems supported facsimile and file transfer, reliability was always an issue.

Then, there was this smartphone thing. At the 1996 CeBIT fair, GSM bellwether Nokia, which had won the handset wars by turning an expensive, gray business tool into a cheap, colorful consumer product, exemplified the nascent wireless data market by introducing the first multipurpose device on a commercial scale. The Nokia 9000 Communicator was a large and pricey product that combined voice telephony with an organizer function and a modest Internet access. Nokia's Communicator had identified the rise of a new segment in the voice-centric wireless industry.

This distinctive palmtop computer-style smartphone was the result of combining a modestly successful and expensive PDA from Hewlett Packard with Nokia's bestselling phone. In fact, the early prototype model had these two particular devices fixed via a hinge. The Nokia 9000—a shotgun marriage of a GSM mobile and a palmtop PDA—had just 8MB of memory and weighed slightly under a pound. It looked like a regular phone from the front until it flipped open to reveal a second screen and a QWERTY keyboard. The handset-cum-organizer made use of an operating system (OS) developed by the California–based company Geoworks Corp. Nokia's Mikko Terho was a leading influence behind the development of arguably the world's first commercial smartphone.

Shortly after this launch, Nokia released an enhanced version with smaller size. The Nokia 9110 Communicator could download web pages during off-peak hours and connect to a digital camera for transmitting pictures. The glitzy device weighing 253 grams got a much publicized product placement in Val Kilmer's 1997 movie *The Saint*. Although 9110 Communicator was an expensive product with a price tag of US$1,000, by enabling services like fax and e-mail on a hybrid platform, it accomplished initial recognition for a new category that could gather momentum in the future. Earlier, to complement such services, Nokia had produced the first cellular data card and software-based data suite for GSM phones.

Apparently, things had started to change with the advent of digital cellular, which significantly reduced the airtime for wireless data traffic, thus helping it to make inroads through viable applications like SMS. With it began wireless industry's quest to redefine itself by marrying data with the voice-centric cellular systems and to make data an integral part of cellular services. It's ironic that at the time GSM was developed—in the late 1980s—many in the mobile communications industry felt that the standard was being over-specified. Critics said that too much capability had been designed into it and that most of it would never be used. By the mid-1990s, just a couple of years after the GSM launch, more than 300 million subscribers had been won, and GSM was not finished yet. The core standard, now well tried and tested, was constantly evolving.

When the work on the standard eventually entered in the third major phase—generally referred to as Phase 2 Plus—the key element of this project catered to data communications that spanned both traditional circuit switching and emerging packet data. The Phase 2 was primarily different from the Phase 1 in having added a number of supplementary services. The functions were organized as a set of independent tasks so that each could be introduced with little or no impact on the others. That approach favored an evolutionary growth path since such independence implied that one network element could be modified without affecting other parts of the system. This proved a decisive turning point in the future growth of the European mobile technology.

The aim of the Phase 2 Plus initiative was to gradually introduce important changes while maintaining upward compatibility with the GSM network. Mobile data—as the GSM designers found out while working on the Phase 2—was the next logical step in the evolution of mobile communications. So the Phase 2 Plus gradually turned into a campaign to preserve GSM competitiveness through the introduction of higher-speed data services. The project took a novel approach to incorporate data services into two modes: High-Speed Circuit Switched Data (HSCSD) and General Packet Radio Service (GPRS).

HSCSD worked by aggregating a number of speech channels into a single pipe comprising a bandwidth of 64 Kbit/s or beyond. Aimed for mission-critical applications due to its support for guaranteed data rate, HSCSD was deemed suitable for constant bit-rate applications such as videoconferencing and telemetry. However, the need to reserve bandwidth for a certain time could become a liability for the overall system. So even before the realization, HSCSD seemed marginalized by the other application, GPRS. Given the IP roots of GPRS and the eminent wireless Internet revolution, the doom of HSCSD became obvious even before it made a foray in the commercial realm. The fate of HSCSD also marked the death of conventional circuit switching technology within the wireless data realm.

Its counterpart, GPRS, was seen as bringing a new lease of life to the dying dream of mobile Internet while it could also facilitate new services in a range of areas from mobile commerce to remote surveillance. As a GSM extension, GPRS used the same channel, same modulation scheme and the same network backbone as HSCSD to offer data-over-cellular services. However, it utilized packet transfer and routing mechanism and optimized airtime by allocating temporary resources for bursty data applications such as Internet access. Inevitably, IP interface and its support for connectionless services attracted special favor in the wake of the rising tide of the Internet usage. GPRS promised to handle data rates flexibly, according to network availability, from modest 9.6 Kbit/s to as much as 144 Kbit/s, and allowed simultaneous voice calls while sending and receiving data.

GPRS STEALS THE SHOW

In many ways, GPRS was recycling of the older American technology, CDPD, in the digital arena—a network overlay requiring additional network cards at base stations that would separate data packets from circuit-switched voice. CDPD had its roots in the analog AMPS world, whereas GPRS belonged to GSM digital cellular technology and was thus perceived to offer better solutions for mobile data applications. This broad distinction was seen as the key factor in GPRS network's ability to push the U.S. mobile data protocol out of the picture altogether. Nevertheless, CDPD continued to play a modest role in providing niche wireless data services in some of the American markets.

The work on GPRS started in 1994, and air interface protocol was proposed after an effort that spanned a period of two years. Ericsson signed the world's first GPRS contract with Deutsche Telekom of Germany in 1999. The network, composed of a switching node and a router, directed data packets to the Internet or any other packet-switched data network. GPRS was going to support almost all the major data communications protocols, including IP, which would enable mobile subscribers to connect directly to any data source. Also, GPRS was designed to work within the existing GSM infrastructure with additional packet switching nodes so that the network coverage could be introduced quickly and easily.

Packet data brought improved spectral efficiency because radio resources in it could be shared simultaneously. Users could remain connected to the accessed data network as long as they wished, but they would be charged only for the actual amount of data transmitted. People no longer had to go through the frustrating dial-up process. Once a connection was made, a user could put the phone down or even make a phone call and then come back to it exactly where he or she had left off. Thanks to GPRS, there was an enormous increase in SMS traffic, while e-mail became an exciting prospect in wireless communications. The GPRS technology seemed to be a practical solution to historical problems of wireless data—cost, bit rate, and user-friendliness.

However, the bigger milestone was that GPRS spec tactfully built itself on top of a successful technology, GSM, while it also adapted to the rapidly changing market needs. GPRS—now widely quoted as the 2.5G wireless network—represented the first implementation of packet switching within GSM, which was essentially a circuit switching technology. The timing could not have been more perfect for GPRS as it quickly became synonymous with the celebrated premise of wireless Internet. GPRS, with its always-on connectivity to the mobile Internet, became a key landmark in the path toward accomplishing broadband mobile Internet juggernaut. The technology that brought much needed packet data capability to mobile communications was now seen as a stepping stone toward the 3G panacea.

Originally, GPRS promised a minimal hardware upgrade to the existing GSM networks and was merely seen as a software upgrade to GSM. However, though its GSM roots enormously helped the technology to achieve widescale industry recognition, the soft launch of GPRS subsequently became an uphill task for the European wireless establishment. There was about ten times as much software involved in a GPRS handset as in a GSM phone. So moving to GPRS could be as much as doing GSM all over again. Nobody was surprised when GPRS was off to a slow start. History would repeat itself when GPRS handsets were nowhere to be seen like the early days of GSM. Following the golden rule of mobile telephony, the GPRS-capable devices were late.

And once these GPRS-enabled phones arrived in the market, they were relatively unaffordable because handsets had only recently acquired multimedia features like color displays and the ability to run downloaded software. This time around, how-ever, the wireless industry was more circumspect in preaching the GPRS gospel. Both wireless operators and manufacturers knew that they faced a potential backlash if they over-promoted GPRS. So the logical first steps were taken without a lot of hype. For a start, they were counting on GPRS to turn around the fate of WAP debacle as accessing the web was quicker with GPRS and the always-on connection was a big advantage for wireless e-mail.

The GPRS network offered higher transmission speed and constant connectivity with minimal use of network resources. And with no dial-up, no drop-off, and speeds of 20 Kbit/s to 40 Kbit/s, it provided a testing ground for the wireless data services. The GSM industry was now envisioning an Internet revival through GPRS networks because an always-on connec-tion coupled with data speeds two to three times faster than before could turn wireless Internet into a viable experience. It also allowed wireless operators to demonstrate that they could market data services. Both in terms of network dynamics like bandwidth and new, souped-up applications, GPRS seemed a prefect precursor to the coming-of-age 3G panorama. It was official now: GPRS was the gateway to 3G.

MOBILE DATA IN TRANSITION

Back in 1999, surfing the Internet on a mobile phone emerged as a very cool idea. However, a couple of years later, waiting several minutes to peer at a few lines of text on a small monochrome screen didn't feel cool at all. Sluggish networks and clunky technology virtually snuffed out most consumers' enthusiasm for the wireless Internet. The industry leaders were concerned that users were fed up with overly hyped wireless Internet services that hadn't met expectations. But now that 2.5G networks were here to rescue the wireless industry, what next? As is the case for many exciting new technologies, it all began with a knee-jerk reaction.

"We still don't know how to use these network capabilities to generate new revenues," acknowledged a spokesman of SK Telecom, the first company in the world to launch commercial 2.5G service in October 2000. SK Telecom, which commanded half of South Korea's mobile subscribers, made the mistake of jumping onto the new-age wireless bandwagon without proper groundwork and was now scrambling to recover. For a country in the vanguard of hot wireless technology, nobody was able to figure out what's going to be on offer in the 2.5G platform. A year since the commercial launch of its 2.5G service, to the frustration of SK Telecom managers, the subscribers were simply talking up against their ears in the traditional fashion.

However, that phase passed rather quickly. Take Blackberry—the first truly successful smartphone—which played a significant part in stimulating the early demand for GPRS networks. The Waterloo, Canada–based firm Research In Motion (RIM), which later renamed itself as Blackberry, for the core product it made, was a pioneer in paging and wireless messaging. The early Blackberry device introduced in 1999 communicated using the low-speed Mobitex network, the one that also provided refuge to the trivial Palm VII launch. It was the launch of the 2.5Gmobile data technology which delivered an always-on connection and allowed data-centric gadgets like Blackberry the ability to jack into the Internet with a faster e-mail connection. RIM reached a wider market in the early 2000s with the launch of GPRS-supported phones like Blackberry 5810 and Blackberry 6210.

The term 2.5G was a media phrase for the group of technologies that used packet switching to deliver data on demand at potential speeds of 144 Kbit/s to 384 Kbit/s. These bridging technologies, also available on other second-generation systems—code-division multiple access (CDMA) and time-division multiple access (TDMA)—were collectively known as 2.5G solutions since they were built on the existing networks using the same transmission frequencies and much of the same equipment. However, because this technology was essentially the second-generation network upgraded to handle data, it was slower than 3G. On the positive side, despite being a long-planned upgrade to the existing wireless phone system, the technology was promising to offer nearly all the benefits of 3G for a fraction of the cost.

During all the fuss over 3G networks, the importance of 2.5G had largely been underplayed. That's partly because the original objective behind 2.5G initiative was about making airwaves wider. But it became evident in the course of time that the very being of 2.5G initiative was crucial for the realization of wireless data services. One of the biggest advantages of 2.5 networks was that data traffic could travel in a channel separate from voice calls. Still, moving from voice to higher speed data and multimedia services was in a stark contrast to the earlier transition carried out to move from analog to digital air interface. This time, the wireless industry was going to grasp a new service platform and a myriad of technology challenges that fell outside its traditional engineering strengths.

The voice-centric wireless communication world was now operating in a new territory—data—and it wasn't an easy turf. And there came the rub. Embracing 2.5G technology wasn't only a matter of the economy or time; it was also indispensable from the learning curve standpoint. A great market experience, GPRS would help make the case for different types of business models; moreover, there was a lot to do in the applications space. The interim step allowed operators to experiment with pricing models and popular data services in anticipation of rolling out the higher-speed 3G networks at a later stage. A slew of new services also allowed wireless operators to start rehearsing 3G applications in an attempt to incite demand. Last but not least, the success with 2.5G provided a vital experience in delivery and billing of wireless data services, which would subsequently help mobile companies master to succeed in 3G business.

However, although the 2.5G initiative looked financially feasible, it wasn't without struggles of its own. The 2.5G technology, because it was a simple network upgrade, was supposed to be quick-and-easy way to get consumers hooked onto the higher-speed data transmission, enabling them to utilize fashionable services such as downloading movie trailers when booking a ticket, or watching sports highlights. However, it was neither easy nor quick. For a start, a key difference between 2.5G and 3G was speed, which translated to the amount of data that could be moved over the spectrum per second. Theoretically, 2.5G would provide speeds of 144 Kbit/s, and 3G should go up to 2 Mbit/s, but these speeds assumed maximum performance that could only be achieved by a stationary user located in a specific coverage area of the network with a few users.

Now service providers began preparing the market for the inevitable disappointment: the bandwidth would be somewhere between 28 Kbit/s to 128 Kbit/s. And as with any shared solution, the more users there were, the less bandwidth they would get. In the final analysis, even 28 Kbit/s was looking awfully optimistic. However, while the video wasn't a sure bet anyway, wireless industry could pioneer ways to beam music and other audio services over 2.5G-enabled phones. After all, cell phone was an audio machine: there was a headphone, a microphone, and selection buttons so users didn't have to change the interface to turn it into, for instance, a music player. At the time when college kids in the United States were downloading music in MP3 format from their personal computers, mobile phone users in Europe and Japan were overjoyed with downloads of ringtone music features.

Then Japanese mobile subscribers, moving a step further, started to download songs directly onto their handsets, which came equipped with headphones. Multimedia messaging service, or MMS, was another bright spot. Its predecessor, SMS, had enjoyed an extraordinary boom by allowing users to send short, telegram-like messages of up to 160 characters from one mobile phone to another. MMS allowed people to send and receive photographs. The industry cheerleaders like Nokia promoted messaging services such as MMS as a critical bridge to 3G wireless technology. They argued that wireless operators should offer a steady stream of improvements to the basic text messaging service—such as the addition of graphics and animation—in order to hold the users' interest and encourage them to migrate gradually to more complex multimedia services.

NEXT STOP 3G

Even though the fate of 2.5G was not clear in the early 2000s, the course of technology that was determined with the emergence of the mobile Internet and multimedia services like MMS had made the process irreversible. The whole idea of 2.5G as a stepping stone to 3G wireless was for real, but there was a dilemma hidden in the bigger scheme of things. If 2.5G didn't work very well, it could really hamper the prospects of 3G. However, if it was too successful, it could steal the thunder from 3G and forestall it indefinitely. Would that mean that 3G networks could be entirely unnecessary in that case? While many analysts claimed that 2.5G was good enough to satisfy everyone's need as far as speed was concerned, mobile phone companies insisted that 2.5G in no way replaced the need for 3G.

Mobile phone operators saw it from a vantage point, and they were right. They argued that 3G would eventually prevail because it was cheaper to operate and that it offered data speeds up to ten times faster than 2.5G, permitting zippy services such as videophones and digital music players. The so-called 2.5G networks provided decent-enough data rates for WAP-based services, but as cell phone browsers matured beyond simple, text-heavy displays, the need arose for a bona fide 3G network capable of handling high-speed data rates. Moreover, the 3G technology was so complex that it would likely arrive years later than promised. And by the time it finally arrived, the 2.5G networks would have become clogged with traffic, and users would be more than willing to switch to 3G for better performance.

Wireless operators had built a great intelligence on voice usage over the decades, but for data, the infrastructure and efforts were generally not on par. Initially, there was little understanding of what consumers were doing, and which applications and services they were tuned to at any given instant. The cost of supporting data services exceeded the cost of managing voice services and the revenues from data services only became prominent after the coming of the iPhone. With the iPhone and credible rivals like Android phones came a growing appetite for data—first in the browser space and later with mobile apps. Case in point: the iPhone was the primary driver behind the unprecedented 5,000 percent increase in data usage on AT&T's network from 2007 to 2010.

Wireless operators now started to pay much more attention to the specifics at a very granular level and formulated business models and pricing plans as per the trends and forecasts. For them, after having started with thin and crispy 2.5G networks, upgrading the capacity to 3G networks was imperative. The advent of smartphones had underscored the need for a specialized network, and there was no looking back. Smartphones, more than any other device, were able to take advantage of these faster networks to empower users to do or access nearly anything. The complete Internet experience that they've had on PC was now available in the mobile space, and that was nothing short of a revolution. The union of ubiquitous high-speed wireless networks with mobile browsers meant people had the power of the web in the palm of their hand.

By 2009, AT&T had been turning heads with the sheer speed of its 3G network. The correlation between the mobile Internet and the 3G networks was evident in the post-iPhone wireless world. The mobile phone industry now had a challenge of wirelessly connecting millions of users to the Internet, and for that, they needed far more capacity than required in providing plain voice services. Smartphones were now into the mainstream, and for this new value proposition, the wireless establishment needed to have faster networks so that they could manage the onslaught of this new gadgetry. The next generation of wireless networks was on its way.

The Nokia 9000 Communicator was probably the first mobile phone with a web browser. It marked the convergence of voice and data on a single device.

Photo courtesy of Nokia

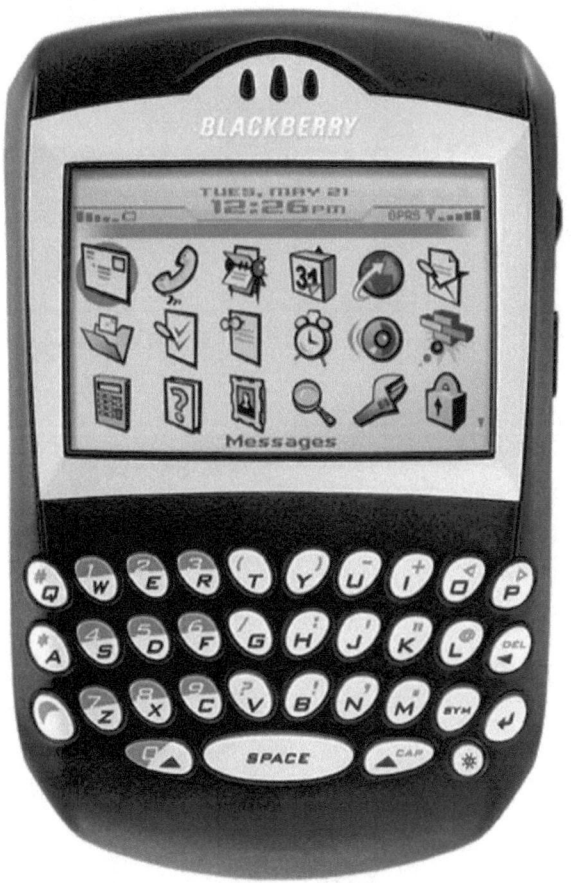

The Blackberry 6210—launched in 2003—was the company's first data device integrated with a phone which put the microphone and speaker inside the device and popularized the nifty scroll wheel. The users had to attach a headset to make calls with the earlier Blackberry 5210 model which came in the market in 2002.

Photo credit: Flickr user Lucia Pimentel

3  THE 3G AFFAIR

"It was early 2007 and we were building our 3G network at that time. We were saying data is going to move to the mobile world. Then you get this device [iPhone] and you go, 'This is it.' Now I can begin to grasp where the mobile world can go with this kind of data device."

—Stephenson Randall, AT&T chief executive officer in an interview with *Forbes* in 2013

Although third-generation wireless or 3G had become a household name by 2010, it took a lot of stops and starts along the way. From its conception in the late 1990s to its worldwide popularity over the following decade, there were some serious hurdles that 3G had to overcome. Start with the early promises of 3G that created a marketing field of dreams in which video would vault mobile phones into an entirely new plane just like the addition of pictures to sound in the new medium of television had transformed broadcasting in the 1950s. The most compelling dimension of 3G, however, was the one that related to the build-out of the next-generation wireless infrastructure for the mobile Internet.

When European planners in Brussels were mapping out the time-table for 3G launch, across the Atlantic, the Internet was moving into the consumer realism and web startups like Netscape had become stock market darlings. Understandably, while piecing together the 3G prototype, Europeans became convinced that the rapid coalescence of mobility and the Internet would crystallize a new market with a powerful and timely convergence. A decade ago, similar central planning for GSM development had helped transform Europe into the world's richest wireless market, turning the regional wireless players, from Nokia to Vodafone, into global powerhouses. So while creating a new continental network—3G—high-speed Internet became Europe's audacious bid to lead the world in a crucial twenty-first-century industry.

For Europeans, it was now a megaproject, the equivalent in size, vision, and expense of America's Apollo space program in the 1960s. This was a unique blend of technological conquest and pervasive market drive borne out of Europe's GSM triumph. The pundits called 3G wireless the vision of the new century, a wireless nirvana where all dreams would come true. The so-called phone of the future riding on 3G platform would be powerful enough to provide high-speed Internet access, video-on-demand and countless whiz-bang features. According to early projections, 3G was to provide users with a whopping 2 Mbit/s of data, more than what most wired offices used to connect their users to the web at that time.

The original hyperbole that the wireless industry had evangelized was that 3G would break bandwidth barriers, bringing Internet access with stereo-quality audio and picture-perfect video to the users' fingertips. A simmering cauldron in this great wireless melodrama was the promise to bring genuine graphical content onto handset displays. The early promises of 3G created a field of dreams, in which a user, for instance, would simply snap a photo, select a name from the address book, and hit the send button. The digital image would instantly pop up on a friend's phone or handheld computer. Video, one of the most eagerly awaited aspects of 3G phones, was another piece of the puzzle that had overwhelmed this initiative from its beginning.

The ability to send and receive photos and video clips over wireless networks had been one of those futurist things the industry talked about in connection with the 3G infrastructure. Now the reality was getting closer to fruition with the arrival of commercial 3G services. They said the time of instant visual communications had come; it was a historic opportunity in the making for a better-connected world. The hype said mobile photo and video applications would blow away the simple messaging and web-clipping services that mobile devices delivered at the time. On the other hand, some skeptical analysts said that videophone history spoke for itself; there was absolutely no market for a mobile videophone.

For decades, futurists had predicted that videophones would become commonplace, but for decades it didn't happen. Videophones first captured the public imagination in 1964 when they were displayed at the World's Fair in New York and tried by the U.S. president's wife Lady Bird Johnson. "A logical extension of today's telephone service," boasted a Bell System advertisement. AT&T and technology journalists alike predicted that videophones would become standard in homes and office within a decade or so. But the idea never took off. That was partly due to the expense of transmitting video signals over long distance; only a handful of people could afford the early videophones. Furthermore, it turned out that most people were not very excited about being seen as they talked on the phone.

Mobile video telephony incorporated a small digital camera on the top of the handset, which sent TV-style color image to other handset's screen. The trouble was that mobility required handsets to be small and light. Even with a color display, tiny screens were still tiny screens. There was a degree of skepticism even within Japan on whether mobile videophones would prove a killer application for 3G wireless. Several Japanese companies had tried to revive mobile videophones with little success. Kyocera, for instance, launched a handset based on Personal Handy-phone System (PHS) cordless technology that transmitted images of the person at the other end of the call. But the company hardly found any takers.

Undeterred, the wireless industry continued to test video prospects. The mobile phone world was hoping to usher in a whole new class of services such as interactive video games and quick music downloads. Analysts speculated that streaming video could become the first popular application for features such as sports highlights and electronic postcards. Despite the technological limitations—tiny screens, jumpy connections, expensive devices, and interminable downloads—plenty of companies believed the demand for delivering photos or streaming videos to handsets was there.

So far video had been jerky because it didn't contain as many frames as a television picture. And transmission rate would eventually fall to as low as 32 Kbit/s. It seemed much like the early days of multimedia PC when people were doing it just because they could and not because it was really useful as an application. The wireless industry had also been slow to develop technology to support multimedia services simply because it was a question of creating a value chain through a radically different content production, which required different knowledge skills from handset manufacturers.

TROUBLE IN PARADISE

The predominantly European mobile phone establishment talked of such killer applications as videoconferencing and other pie-in-the-sky schemes that kept service providers and manufacturers busily plotting about how they would get into the act. But the 2 Mbit/s claim was not realistic in the first place because the keyword "shared" was almost always omitted from the boastful projections. Worse still, the ugly truth was that many service providers couldn't even provide 2 Mbit/s solutions in the near term but instead would satisfy market needs with a mere 384 Kbit/s. Again, this bandwidth would be shared among all users within a particular cell.

The NTT DoCoMo and British Telecom (BT) rollouts in 2001, launched in a rush to become the world's first company to offer 3G services, showcased not only the shortcomings of the new technology but also the challenges that merely came with the first-mover status. Although both companies attributed the delays to software glitches, the Japanese and the Isle of Man rollouts offered the world a glimpse of the deployment issues as well as of the complexity and newness of 3G technology. Consumer acceptance also failed to match the launch-day hype. DoCoMo could sell only 42,000 3G handsets, far fewer than 150,000 phones target the company had modestly projected to achieve by March 2002. Third-generation handsets cost three to five times as much as conventional phones. They were clumsy and glitch-prone and had a relatively short battery life.

Spotty coverage, high prices, and shorter battery life of handsets continued to stifle the DoCoMo and BT services. Meanwhile, European operators either delayed or shelved plans to roll out 3G after spending about US$100 billion on government licenses for the services. Now that DoCoMo and BT had taken the plunge with 3G, Deutsche Telekom's then-chairman Rolf Sommer said his company wouldn't launch commercial services until it was satisfied that the network was robust and working to the existing high-quality standards, and that suitable handsets and applications were ready. Similar views were echoed by the American wireless stalwart Motorola, who correctly figured out that the actual 3G rollout would kick off in 2004, followed by widescale deployment in 2005.

The original premise was rather too simple: beef up the wireless networks, and users will flock to them to browse the web, send e-mails with mile-long attachments, and even download video clips all on their phones. The execution proved to be a giant technical and financial challenge, however. Content and applications were clearly not ready yet, but every telecom outfit was standing in the line, saying that if 3G wireless took off, it should not be the one left behind. The perception of data services had been driven more by the wireless industry's enthusiasm than by the market demand. Moreover, piping voice and data through a single converged handset required complex new partnerships among wireless, Internet, and a myriad of other service companies.

No one had actually figured out how to share the work let alone the revenue. There was no clear business plan; multinational giants jumped onto the 3G bandwagon with no more of a clue than barroom ideas of dotcom flameouts. Another important lesson from this mobile extravagance was that there is never enough bandwidth, so one must focus on technology that optimizes the use of bandwidth. The telecommunications industry had long been a victim of the myth that bandwidth was everything. But a mere progression in speed could be meaningless in many ways because what applications did at the desktop was substantially different from what they did on a cell phone. The i-mode example had affirmed that mobile phone companies needed to think about making attractive offers to end-users instead of merely relying on fancy marketing campaigns.

Whether data services would generate sufficient revenue was also open to question in the early going. Would people really want to download high-bandwidth applications, such as video clips, to the tiny screens of mobile phones? No one was sure. And no one yet knew what the killer application might be to capture the imagination of people and hence turn 3G into a moneymaker. Still, with an exciting new technology on the horizon, wireless companies felt they had no choice but to jump in.

TOO LITTLE TOO SOON

The 3G wireless story became a mystic tale of another technology debacle. What distinguished 3G mania from the dotcom bubble—which burst in the same time periphery—was the size of its victims and their ambitions: they were not little startups, but the world's major telecommunications operators and manufacturers. How did this happen? In hindsight, it's easy to see why so many successful companies fell to the allure of 3G. An industry that grew fat on the booming cell phone business had to rush to master new specialties: Internet services and smartphones. While the cost and risk of 3G were frightening, the alternative for such high-flying firms as Ericsson and Orange of learning to live with near-saturated mobile-voice markets and declining user revenues would have been even worse.

When the high-tech bubble burst, Carl Yankowski, a consumer electronics industry veteran and then-CEO of Palm Inc., compared 3G to the HDTV saga of the 1980s. Intel's Hans Geyer, while speaking at the 2001 GSM World Congress in Cannes, France went a step further when he told attendees that the wireless industry was heading for bankruptcy before even a single 3G call was made. The technology press quickly scaled down 3G to small talk, and the focus turned away from 3G toward tangible applications such as ringtones and camera phones. The mobile phone industry nevertheless maintained its relentless pursuit of advancements through user appetite for multimedia-rich features.

It's easy to overdo the pessimism. While a majority of industry analysts decried the lethargy in 3G, a group of cheerleaders still believed it was the only way forward. Third-generation wireless was about a new paradigm, they said, which needed to adapt to a radically different world, and it couldn't happen overnight. In the long term, 3G could prove a boon, but it would take time. These evangelists reminded doomsayers, on the other side of the fence, that GSM was not an instant success either; it too had its teething problems. Even text messaging found a lukewarm response in its early years. The apparent shift toward multimedia services, they said, favored 3G, whose bigger transmission pipes required rich content to justify new applications.

Everybody knew wireless bandwidth was a hodgepodge, so problems were bound to erupt. To some industry observers, the rhetoric about 3G fallout was reminiscent of the early days of GSM when people said whatever digital offered could be done with analog. After all, voice is analog, these critics used to argue. A more granular view of this whole episode revealed that what really had bitten the dust was not 3G itself but overhyped visions of its potential.

In retrospect, the optimists were right. For 3G, one of the biggest gambles in business history, payback came in rather strange ways. First, the transformation from 2G to 3G was evolution- ary and would take several years. A full suite of voice and data offerings would eventually make the transition from 2.5G to 3G inevitable anyway. Second, multimedia-messaging services like MMS, which evolved from SMS, subsequently played a key role in driving the network rollout. Such services would allow downloads of ringtones for mobile phones in stereo or MIDI files along with video clips and animations. People could send and receive non-real-time transmission of text synchronized with audio and video images over cell phones. Third, despite this maze of sophisticated data services, voice remained the real breadwinner for mobile phone operators.

In an ironic twist, voice came forward to provide a safety net for the shaky 3G start. At one stage, it looked as if the focus of 3G would move away from commercially unproven multimedia services, such as videoconferencing, toward providing extra capacity for voice traffic. The existing cellular networks were already approaching full capacity as users continued exodus from fixed to mobile networks. In pure voice terms, 3G networks would offer at least twenty times the capacity of the existing GSM networks. In theory, an operator could go on creating extra capacity by splitting cells in the GSM system, but the wireless industry was reaching a point where it would be more costly to do this than build a new 3G network.

The 3G story started with an optimism that became the hallmark of the wireless communication's vision for the twenty-first century. Then pessimism followed, creating shock waves throughout the mobile phone world. However, once the cycle of boom and gloom was over, the new buzzword was realism that said, "3G is here, taking one step forward on its course, and that it's based on some real business case." Now there was more awareness on difficulties ahead and on the need to create new business models and revenue streams.

Third-generation wireless was likely to cost an operator several billion dollars, and many years to roll out a complete network. Plus, 3G coverage could remain spotty and sporadic for years. But the wheels of history wouldn't go backward. After the days of blind faith in this mobile enigma ended, 3G was still standing as the only viable solution for the longer term. Although the elusive quest for an unprecedented wireless glory was over, the future 3G landscape was starting to take shape nevertheless. After early alarm bells, by 2002, network construction was well under way, albeit at a slower pace than predicted earlier. Buying into 3G would mean buying a promise: wait a few more years, and buying the real thing would become more likely.

That real thing came by in the late 2000s when the iPhone and Android pushed the mobile Internet well into the mainstream with hundreds of millions of subscribers. The wireless industry—then focused on voice and messaging services—was caught unguarded by the explosive growth in mobile Internet traffic. For them, data was only useful to the mobile enterprise workers and early adopters who used smartphones with clunky browsers that made mobile web surfing far less appealing. But Apple's seductive phone with its powerful software and intuitive interface encouraged users to go online and stay online. The iPhone users consumed an average of up to ten times the bandwidth of mobile subscribers. They were playing games on their phones, sending video messages, or downloading music. A new network regime was taking shape in a wireless order created by smartphones like the iPhone.

EVOLUTION, NOT REVOLUTION

Despite setbacks, on both technological and marketing fronts, wireless industry's commitment to deploy 3G remained unshaken. The wireless companies picked up the pieces and began to work out the kinks for providing quality phones that would subsequently accompany this new technology. Once 3G began to take hold, cell phone companies worked tirelessly to find ways to utilize this new technology. Although mobile phones long had the ability to access data networks such as the

Internet, it was not until the widespread availability of good-quality 3G coverage in the mid-2000s that specialized devices like the iPhone emerged to access the mobile Internet. As coffee-shop goers and technology experts alike attested the speed was completely real.

The wireless industry didn't see meaningful deployment of 3G networks until 2003 in Japan, 2004 in Europe, and 2005 in the United States. In the start, while 3G was in its infancy, still-slow GSM networks evolved even further from GPRS to a zippier technology dubbed as Enhanced Data Rates for GSM Evolution, or EDGE for short. The preferred U.S. version read EDGE as Enhanced Data Rates for Global Evolution. The EDGE technology (GSM 384 specification) was originally developed by Ericsson for operators with no Universal Mobile Telecommunications System (UMTS) spectrum; EDGE enabled both GSM and TDMA operators to offer data services at speeds closer to those available at UMTS-based 3G networks.

In fact, in the early stages, the GSM-centric evolution path to 3G in the predominantly European UMTS technology had left the U.S. TDMA operators like AT&T Wireless in the cold. So they had little choice but to embrace EDGE before moving on to an entirely new 3G technology: UMTS based on wideband-CDMA air interface. The interest in EDGE initially came from the United States also because it wasn't bitten by the 3G spectrum blues. Otherwise, despite EDGE's ability to support 384 Kbit/s—up from 144 Kbit/s via GPRS—and the fact that EDGE cost a fraction of a 3G network, the cash-starved wireless operators long ignored this technology. The first EDGE network was rolled out by Cingular Wireless in 2003 with theoretical speeds reaching 236.8 Kbit/s, though in reality it reached nowhere near that.

The EDGE network delivered higher bit rate per channel and offered a three-fold increase in capacity and performance compared to GPRS connections. It required a relatively minor software and hardware upgrade on the base station side, and was less expensive to build into handsets and other devices. It was an unsung hero of the 3G tale, and its rise to the occasion was a testament to 3G's evolutionary journey. It's worthwhile to mention that Apple's very first iPhone had been launched on AT&T's EDGE network. The EDGE standard brought an immediate solution for higher-speed data services to TDMA/GSM operators and its proximity with GPRS was surely helpful. Some industry folks even called EDGE a 2.75G technology.

The 3G bandwagon moved from EDGE network to the UMTS standard, and then to various flavors of paired High Speed Downlink Packet Access (HSDPA) and HSUPA (the U for Uplink). HSDPA rates commonly deployed were 3.6 Mbit/s, 7.2 Mbit/s, 14 Mbit/s, and 21 Mbit/s depending on the network; HSUPA rates ran from 1.5 Mbit/s to 6 Mbit/s on the upstream. Further refinements to the UMTS-based 3G technology would produce HSPA+, dual-carrier HSPA+, and HSPA+ Evolution, ranging in theoretical speeds from 14 Mbit/s to a mind-boggling 600 Mbit/s. On the CDMA front, the Qualcomm-backed cdma2000 standard got a nifty software upgrade to EV-DO systems with Rev. A and Rev. B specs. The EV-DO Rev. A 3G network topped out at 3.1 Mbit/s downstream and 1.8 Mbit/s upstream.

The UMTS-based 3G standard was built around the Third Generation Partnership Project (3GPP) which structured specifications as Releases. Specifications from 3GPP—a global telecommunications consortium comprising of members in most GSM dominant countries—were based on the GSM evolution path. The two basic building blocks in the UMTS-based 3G fabric—radio access network (RAN) and core network—were kept entirely separate and independent of each other. The core network architecture of UMTS was based on GSM/GPRS legacy systems while the RAN part utilized the wideband CDMA technology for the 3G air interface.

The Release 5 from 3GPP launched the HSDPA specification which introduced packet-based data services to UMTS in the same way that GPRS did for the GSM standard. The completion of packet data for UMTS was achieved in Release 6 with the addition of High Speed Uplink Packet Access or HSUPA. HSDPA and HSUPA were collectively known as High Speed Packet Access (HSPA). Then came the Release 7, High Speed Packet Access Plus (HSPA+), which employed a multiple-antenna technique for improved system performance, high-efficiency modulation technique for extra capacity and improved packet efficiency, and continuous packet connectivity (CPC) functionality for reducing power consumption of mobile devices.

The subsequent standard or Release 8 was Long Term Evolution (LTE), which was based on orthogonal frequency-division multiplexing (OFDM) and multiple-input multiple-output (MIMO) techniques. The LTE technology was soon adopted by major wireless operators like Vodafone, Verizon, and NTT DoCoMo. Eventually, LTE became a candidate for the fourth-generation wireless (4G) standard.

In the United States, for 3G deployment, Verizon and Sprint had opted for CDMA-based systems, also referred to as EV-DO, while GSM followers AT&T and T-Mobile used an enhanced version of 3G technology: HSDPA. A speedier version—HSPA+ or Turbo

3G—boasted download speeds of up to 14 Mbit/s. The fact of the matter was that the 3G wireless standard was largely defined not by the underlying technology but by its speed.

The 3G affair, sparked by the promised merger of voice and data onto cellular handset, started reaching critical mass by the late-2000s. First, wireless networks became more economical to deploy after some years of manufacture and costs dropped for both 3G base stations and handsets. At around the same time, the emergence of dual-core processors allowed handsets to offload much of the work to a separate application processor, which inevitably helped 3G takeoff. The technology's reputation as a power hog also eased after handset designers adopted new power-management techniques to optimize battery life. Meanwhile, memory capacity kept increasing to support new features. During the mid-2000s, an average handset carried 4 MB of storage; within two to three years, memory capacities had surpassed 64 MB mark.

According to a study from Statistic Brain, by 2012, there were 1,594 million 3G mobile users across the world, enjoying the path to mobile TV, video communications, and location-based services. Still, the 3G-based mobile Internet had turned into one big traffic jam, and unlike wired Internet, where more bandwidth meant laying more fiber cables and adding more servers, there was only so much bandwidth that mobile carriers could squeeze form the available spectrum. Not surprisingly, therefore, AT&T discontinued unlimited data provision and migrated to the capped data plans only two years after launching the iPhone in 2007. Verizon's unlimited data plans only lasted for a few months following its iPhone launch in 2011.

Around the world, wireless operators such as O2 in Britain and SingTel in Singapore were facing similar struggles. Moreover, by 2010, with the availability of media savvy devices such as iPad hooked onto wireless networks, it had become evident that at some point 3G networks would be overwhelmed by the growth of bandwidth-intensive applications like video streaming. So the wireless industry began looking for data-optimized technologies with the promise of speed improvements up to tenfold over the existing 3G technologies.

The next step was inevitably 4G. However, before digging deep into the 4G phenomenon, the book will cover the complementary relationship between mobile networks and Wi-Fi. Smartphone—among other things—could log into Wi-Fi networks seamlessly. The rise of the smartphone meant an exponential growth in data use, and here at this crossroads, the nearly ubiquitous Wi-Fi networks quickly emerged as a welcome offloading solution to the mobile data crunch. The Wi-Fi hotspots were able to seamlessly transition a mobile user between the cellular and Wi-Fi networks without any service interruption.

Shin-Ichai Kanai of NEC's Telecom Modus subsidiary and Manx Telecom managing director Chris Hall share some happy moments during the mobile video demo in which NEC's palm-sized image viewer terminal was connected to a 3G handset. British Telecom became a 3G pioneer when it rolled out one of the first 3G services on the Isle of Man through its subsidiary Manx Telecom in 2001. That made the tiny self-governing British territory in the middle of Irish Sea a part of the power struggle for the future of 3G wireless.

Photo: *Microwave Engineering Europe*

Steve Jobs and Stan Sigman at a dinner hosted by the Wireless History Foundation; Sigman orchestrated AT&T's 3G-centric partnership with Apple for the launch of the iPhone, which changed the wireless industry forever.

Coracle Group LLC photo

4 THE REAL WIRELESS INTERNET

"Absolutely anyone can be a Wi-Fi operator."

—Dave Fraser, CEO, Devicescape Software Inc.

The book has shed light on how mobile handsets were primed for video in the age of 3G wireless and how exciting moment this was in the mobile technology evolution. That, however, also led to fears that casual scans of YouTube clips and streams of Netflix movie downloads could crush cellular networks. Moreover, gulping gigabytes of bandwidth for high-definition movie streams could also eat through mobile consumers' wallets and disrupt wireless operators' data plans. Here, Wi-Fi came to rescue the dream of adoption of rich content on smartphones through intelligent and predictive models, which called for automatic detection when a mobile device hit a Wi-Fi network and started downloading content such as movies and e-books. The fact that Wi-Fi was cheaper and faster than cellular networks made it a crucial deterrent against the strains of graphic and video communications.

Most smartphones offered by AT&T had built-in Wi-Fi, which let the handset automatically switch from the cellular network to a Wi-Fi hotspot without a need for prompting. Mobile consumers could use their devices on Wi-Fi networks, including those at more than thirty thousand AT&T Wi-Fi hotspots in the United States, without counting against their monthly data allotments. Hotspots were generally fee-based Wi-Fi access points for a public place like a coffee shop. The hybrid phones let people make connections using a local Wi-Fi access point and seamlessly switch over to a cell phone network once outside the hotspot. The net result was greater flexibility in mobile communications as well as potential cost savings gained by shifting data usage minutes from cell phone plan onto the Wi-Fi-based local wireless network.

Wi-Fi has a fascinating history. In 1980, an engineer named Michael Marcus proposed the idea of opening up the 900 MHz industrial, science and medical (ISM) band at 2.4 GHz and 5.8 GHz frequencies. Marcus theorized that license-free radio spectrum in the hands of technology entrepreneurs would stimulate innovation and thus yield productive benefits. After five years of prodding from Marcus, in 1985, the Federal Communications Commission (FCC) opened up the so-called garbage band allocated for household devices like microwave ovens and radio-controlled toy cars. However, the commission mandated that this new license-free band would use spread spectrum technology to ensure that there was no interference with the existing devices using the ISM band. Spread spectrum technology distributed radio signals over multiple frequencies for secure and interference-free communications.

In those days, IT equipment maker NCR Corp. faced a problem: its retail customers changed their floor plan from time to time, and when they did that, the NCR-provided cash registers had to move and be re-connected to the computer servers. So in 1988, NCR, which wanted to use the unlicensed radio spectrum to hook up its wireless cash registers, asked Victor Hayes to look into this technology prospect. The engineering teams of NCR and its joint venture partner AT&T eventually developed the Wi-Fi technology in 1991 in Neuwegein, the Netherlands. The product called WaveLAN—offering speeds of 1 Mbit/s to 2 Mbit/s—would serve cashier systems in a wireless environment.

Hayes, along with Bruce Tuch of Bell Labs, subsequently approached the Institute of Electrical and Electronics Engineers (IEEE), where a committee named 802.3 had earlier developed the Ethernet LAN standard. Consequently, a new committee called 802.11 was formed, and work on a new wireless LAN standard began. Hayes was the first chair of the IEEE 802.11 group, which in 1997 finalized the wireless standard that later became known to the world as Wi-Fi. The Netherlands native, who had joined NCR in 1974, is often being referred to as the "Father of Wi-Fi" for his role in establishing and chairing the IEEE 802.11 Standards Working Group for Wireless LANs.

Hayes, a senior research fellow at the Delft University of Technology, led the IEEE 802.11 committee through its first decade. In 2003, Hayes retired from Agere Systems, a semiconductor offshoot from telecom equipment maker Lucent Technologies, which in turn, had spun off from telecommunications conglomerate

AT&T. Bruce Tuch was another tech luminary prominent in the making of the Wi-Fi technology. After his early contribution in the development of WaveLAN product and technology standardization at IEEE 802.11 committee, he continued to lead the Wi-Fi development efforts at the Agere System's Utrecht Systems Engineering Centre in the Netherlands.

Wi-Fi MANIA

The name Wi-Fi was coined by brand consulting firm Interbrand Corp. as a catchier replacement of the otherwise tech-heavy nomenclature. Wi-Fi was short for wireless fidelity. Over the years, the Wi-Fi Alliance—the non-profit organization formed in 1999 to certify interoperability of IEEE 802.11-based wireless LAN products—accomplished something truly remarkable: it turned Wi-Fi into a tech brand recognized across the world. The term Wi-Fi eventually became synonymous with wireless LAN products that were compatible with the IEEE 802.11 standards.

Early developers like Proxim and Symbol created their own company-specific products and their wireless LAN equipment didn't communicate with another company's equipment. As a result, Wi-Fi customers were locked into buying from one particular supplier, and that put severe restraints on the commercial viability of Wi-Fi products. Then there came a breakthrough. In 1998, when Steve Jobs returned to Apple as CEO, he engaged Lucent Technologies to incorporate Wi-Fi technology into Apple's upcoming iBook notebook computers at a reasonable price point. Jobs wanted Lucent to deliver the Wi-Fi radio card for

US$50 which Apple would sell for US$99. Lucent came through on its end of the bargain, and Apple introduced the new wireless card as AirPort in its iBook lineup launched in 1999. Other computer makers were quick to notice the trend and adopted the new Wi-Fi technology in their laptops.

The early 2000s saw an unstoppable grassroots movement to deploy Wi-Fi in business and public access points, attempting to recreate the Internet in the wireless space all over again. Folks began calling it the real wireless Internet. The office version of Wi-Fi was widely adopted in the U.S. market while the rest of the world caught up with that over time. Public Wi-Fi, on the other hand, targeted small user segments while offering wireless Internet service to indoor locations such as at cafés, airports, and campuses. That was followed by an era in which Wi-Fi was about in-home PC connectivity. A small wireless router was merely hooked into the existing wired Internet connection at home and people could take their notebooks within home wherever they pleased. The sense of being unwired was exhilarating.

However, Wi-Fi networks became nearly ubiquitous when cellular systems became overburdened with the advent of smartphone devices like the iPhone and Wi-Fi made up for that bandwidth crunch in home and public venues. Wi-Fi marked a promising inflection point at a time when 3G had stumbled, inspiring a mania that was unseen since the great Internet boom of 1990s. No wonder, Wi-Fi turned into a poster child for pervasive computing—another manifestation of always-on computing—and became the undoing of a tradition of controlled use of bandwidth in the wireless world. Wi-Fi eventually became wireless data's second silver bullet after SMS.

During this time, some watchers in the computer industry began asking who needed 3G anyway. In fact, in the early stages, cellular carriers, who had spent billions of dollars to upgrade their systems for high-speed 3G networks, were also skeptical to integrate Wi-Fi and cellular into a single package. In the early going, mobile phone operators in general considered Wi-Fi as an evil incarnate—free, unlicensed spectrum they couldn't charge. In the hindsight, however, Wi-Fi wasn't a 3G replacement as some people in the computer industry had dreamed, but was an appendage to 3G networks. Wi-Fi was a short-range wireless technology that couldn't provide the blanket coverage of a mobile network. While 3G was mobile, Wi-Fi was nomadic.

Here, it's worthwhile to mention that the early versions of Wi-Fi cell phones failed miserably because of the enormous drain on batteries and because users were forced to manually switch between networks. Wireless operator's fetish with accounting and billing systems was another major hurdle in the way of widescale Wi-Fi acceptance. But then Motorola solved the automatic transfer problem by allowing the cell phone sense when it was about to reach the end of the Wi-Fi coverage. While the connection still traveled through the Wi-Fi network, the phone would register the connection onto cellular network, in essence creating a second phone line for the link.

Wireless operators began to treat Wi-Fi as an extension of their cellular networks only after the initial knee-jerk reaction. Despite the fact that Wi-Fi was touted as a 3G killer in the early phase of its success, after Apple's iPhone launch, it became an important complement to 3G networks and accomplished broad industry recognition. Now almost every mobile phone operator had a "Wi-Fi offload" plan to satisfy mobile data traffic and hold down the cost of building cellular capacity.

What's critical was to make Wi-Fi seamless with cellular networks. The Wi-Fi industry, on its part, had started negotiating the tricky connection between the phone and Wi-Fi access point without messing around with log-ins and registration pages as part of its Hotspot 2.0 and Passpoint initiatives. If a device was authorized to use a particular hotspot on an operator's network, it simply connected. A Wi-Fi access point became just another cell on the cellular operator's network: data sessions and even voice calls could be passed from the cellular to Wi-Fi connection. While Hotspot 2.0 was about certifying the hotspot itself, providing authentication using SIMs or certificates, the Passpoint initiative ensured that mobile phones could log into Wi-Fi networks seamlessly.

Then, there was the Next Generation Hotspot (NGH) standard which boasted support from some of the world's biggest operators, including AT&T, China Mobile, BT, NTT DoCoMo and Orange. This industry initiative would enable complex roaming arrangements among cellular carriers and Wi-Fi network service providers. The NGH standard would help negotiate the multi-level roaming agreements, allowing devices to not only connect to multiple networks seamlessly but also prioritize which networks they connect to. The technology went into the trial phase in 2012 and eventually moved to the deployment mode in fall 2013.

THE iPHONE EFFECT

One of Apple's radical efforts in the smartphone arena was the effective integration of Wi-Fi into the cellular mainstream. The iPhone's touchscreen interface fascinated gadget enthusiasts, and so did the Wi-Fi capability, the software, and the multitude of applications. Apple forced mobile carriers to seriously consider handsets with Wi-Fi capability. Mobile phone carriers, who didn't want to have anything to do with Wi-Fi, were now coming around to Wi-Fi as an optional feature recognizing the inevitability. The iPhone really reinvigorated the ability to use both kinds of networks on a single device and allowed consumers to take advantage of the best each had to offer. Ironically, the U.S. mobile phone operators had also been resisting the introduction of touchscreen handsets, saying they wouldn't work in the United States.

The iPhone liaison with AT&T had led to the first meaningful Wi-Fi integration into the mobile phone world. Then in 2010, at the launch of the iPhone 4, Apple raised Wi-Fi's strategic value once more by moving FaceTime-based video calling service onto Wi-Fi networks exclusively. Now, after Apple showed them the way, the mobile phone establishment was finally angling to join the Wi-Fi movement. The cell phone service providers had started signing roaming agreements with hotspot companies in anticipation of more widespread use of Wi-Fi in cell phones. The key players from both the cellular operator community and the Wi-Fi ecosystem had actively come together and supported each other for this industry-wide thrust.

Clearly, when it came to mobile data, smartphone users were far more reliant on Wi-Fi than 3G wireless. The Wi-Fi technologies could support more capacity at a much lower cost. According to a 2012 report from wireless consultant Richard Thanki, a cellular picocell cost from US$7,500 to US$15,000 whereas a much higher capacity carrier-grade Wi-Fi access point cost around US$2,000. Moreover, the cost of a Wi-Fi chipset for a consumer device was around US$5, whereas 3G cellular chipsets cost around US$30. Apparently, the high costs of mobile data transport and cellular hardware had already made Wi-Fi a much preferable alternative to mobile broadband. Furthermore, mobile phone operators could implement Wi-Fi resources without getting bogged down in the hassles of licensing additional spectrum.

AT&T, for example, had acquired or set up thirty thousand of its own hotspots, including at McDonald's and Starbucks stores and was rolling out free coverage in twenty parks in New York City. Interestingly, the city itself had been installing more Wi-Fi networks at schools, libraries and senior centers. In fact, New York City had a pilot program to add Wi-Fi transmitters to more than twelve thousand old-fashioned payphones. According to a research report by Berg Insight, a Gothenburg, Sweden–based market research firm, wireless operators had deployed more than 7 million carrier-grade Wi-Fi access points worldwide by the end of 2012. And by 2018, according to Berg Insight forecasts, the number was going to more than double to about 15 million Wi-Fi access points.

Mobile phone operators could ease the spectrum crunch simply by getting rid of as much data traffic as possible and offloading it to Wi-Fi networks provided either through their own hotspots or by external service providers like AirSense, WeFi, and Towerstream. Here, the question arose: what was the free Wi-Fi payback? From AT&T to New York City to Towerstream, mobile ad revenues were the common thread in enabling free Wi-Fi services for consumers. Firms like Towerstream, for instance, were providing sponsored Wi-Fi services for users willing to view a selection of daily deals.

Then, there were Wi-Fi equipment makers like Ruckus Wireless and BelAir Networks—later acquired by Ericsson—which were not only building small cells that paired Wi-Fi and LTE together as access technologies, but they were also using Wi-Fi mesh architectures to backhaul those cells. Ericsson's purchase of the metro Wi-Fi vendor BelAir Networks was a clear sign that the wireless operators now wanted to integrate Wi-Fi as a standard access means into their mobile networks. Not surprisingly, therefore, wireless equipment makers of telecom origin like Ericsson were increasingly looking to integrate Wi-Fi technology more deeply into their mobile network portfolios.

Wi-Fi being an in-building technology worked very well in indoor and urban environments. Pairing free Wi-Fi with location-based services improved the business proposition and opened up new revenue streams in crowded locations such as hotels and shopping malls. Inevitably, the companies that developed or operated Wi-Fi networks had a new pitch for retailers and marketers: use technology to keep tabs on customers. Places like stores, malls, and airports had started installing Wi-Fi networks to please smartphone-toting users, who used them to get faster Internet access and avoid cellular-data charges. In return, Wi-Fi technology let the network operator keep tabs on what users were doing—from where they were standing to what websites they were visiting. For instance, retailers could learn in what aisle shoppers were most likely to point their smartphone browser to Amazon. com.

That provided mall owners with a new means to judge which storefronts attracted the most foot traffic. Moreover, owners of Wi-Fi networks could turn their antennas into virtual billboards, charging a premium for ads sent to users' phones in prime locations. The smartphone industry had started taking advantage of location as an information source and as a way of creating a richer experience, which was one way to overcome the limitations of the smaller screen. A new breed of startups had started to frantically work on the technologies that would enable additional services such as location-finding in emergency, location-based push advertising, and location-based service listings. These upstarts offered location-based services in the realm of travel, entertainment, and restaurant recommendations.

There was a word of caution, though. The popularity of Groupon and other discount sites was a testament that consumers craved for deals. However, the challenge was in offering the deals without compromising security and violating privacy. Mobile users didn't want six different offers within the span of ten minutes. Network service providers or their customers, such as retailers, must not push any deal or coupon pop-up until mobile users were idle and they must ensure that the deal or coupon was contextually relevant to the mobile user needs. Second, trying to knowingly or unknowingly capture private data about smartphone users could backfire, so service providers operating in the Wi-Fi environment must refrain from mining personal user data through privacy-invading apps.

Moreover, there had to be a level of transparency where consumers clearly knew when they were sharing their location and with whom. Apple and Google, for instance, collected location data from mobile devices to ensure efficient switching between cellular networks and Wi-Fi hotspots. So it's quite plausible that for the right product experiences, most mobile consumers would be willing to share their location, giving the Wi-Fi operators and the developers of location applications a goldmine of data to explore. However, people want the ability to control what offers they receive, and when they receive them, whether through opt-in or check-in or preference-type settings. Well aware that privacy concerns could be a land mine, many of the companies aiming to capitalize on location services were now developing necessary safeguards to protect their subscribers. The purpose of these location services is to be of value to customers, and we are certainly not going to do anything they don't want, they said.

The smartphone explosion inevitably meant an exponential growth in data use and Wi-Fi was the key offloading venue that the mobile industry could monetize along with the upcoming 4G networks. However, the mobile establishment needed to be circumspect in its dealing with Wi-Fi deployments at a larger scale. While Wi-Fi networks were readily available at airports, hotels and some public places, paying for Wi-Fi service at most of these places not only took money out of consumers' pockets, it was also a kind of distraction and a time hassle. Wi-Fi had been so popular mainly because it was easy-to-use and almost free. Mobile operators' consumer surveys showed that even a simple "terms and conditions" pop-up on their Wi-Fi hotspot service caused a 50 percent drop-off rate because mobile users considered this as an inconvenience.

Unlimited data plans from mobile phone operators weren't likely to make a comeback. At the same time, however, it was imperative that the mobile data price per gigabyte come down incrementally. Since the time when Apple had kicked off the mobile-data revolution with the launch of the first 3G iPhone in 2008 and the average data consumption skyrocketed, there was an underlying expectation that data cost would fall as usage ramped up. Otherwise, it was plausible that companies like Apple would take their revolution somewhere else. There were already some indicators. For instance, the vast majority of iPad owners used their tablets solely over Wi-Fi connections. In the twilight world of cellular and Wi-Fi, it was evident by now that Wi-Fi and 4G would go hand in hand in the next phase of the wireless revolution.

Michael Marcus (left), who proposed the idea of free ISM frequency band back in 1980, is pictured here with another wireless pioneer Victor Hayes at Mount Vernon after the Wi-Fi History Conference in April 2008. Hayes is often being referred to as the "Father of Wi-Fi" for his role in establishing and chairing the IEEE 802.11 committee for the wireless LAN standard.

Photo courtesy of Marcus Spectrum Solutions LLC

Bruce Tuch (third from the left) was another lead innovator in the Wi-Fi development arena; the photo was taken during the second IEEE Workshop on wireless LANs being held at the Worcester Polytechnic Institute in October 1996.

Photo credit: Worcester Polytechnic Institute

5 ALL DATA 4G NETWORK

"The iPhone is going to be the first big catalyst for adoption of LTE."

—Murali Nemani, director of
marketing at Cisco Systems

Internet downloads and GPS position finding could be accomplished with 3G speeds but *Dick Tracy*-style video calling could not, at least not without significant compression techniques. Then there were applications like music and games that continued to grow at a rapid pace, making it imperative for the wireless establishment to ensure that bandwidth stays ahead of customer demand, now and in the future. As the saying goes "out with the old, in with the new," such was the case with 3G networks gradually making way for mobile Internet-centric fourth-generation wireless systems commonly known as 4G, the network that promised to be faster, stronger, and overall better than its predecessor. Wireless companies hoped that 4G would revolutionize the way people connect to the Internet. They even anticipated that 4G would eliminate the need for smartphones to search for Wi-Fi hotspots in order to connect to the high-speed Internet.

The average data usage per device was on the rise, and so was the total number of connected devices each person owned. Moreover, not only were the number of smartphones and tablets increasing, but more devices from cameras to cars were getting connected to the mobile juggernaut. According to estimates from Cisco Systems Inc., in 2012, there were 4.3 billion mobile subscribers, and a little less than a billion would add up to this figure by 2017. The top networking gearmaker had predicted that worldwide mobile data traffic would increase thirteen-fold between 2012 and 2017. The continued growth in mobile traffic would continue to be driven by the increase in mobile devices and wireless machine-to-machine connections. It's worth noting that video represented over 50 percent of mobile data traffic in 2012 and it would grow to 66 percent of all mobile traffic within the next five-year period.

The turbo-speed 4G networks promised to fulfill the long-held technology dream where smartphones were going to rival personal computers by bringing the broadband Internet speeds to mobile environments. The 4G wireless technology was a whole new ballgame and old 3G rules that determined which mobile operators were blessed with iPhones devices didn't apply here. However, in some ways, the so-called "4G" network of 2013 resembled the 3G network of 2001. Mobile users could stream extremely high-quality video and upload huge files in the blink of an eye—given the right circumstances.

In retrospect, 3G became a catch phrase which was very much part of the aphorism celebrating the long-awaited arrival of the smartphone. And now a handy, easy-to-grasp way of referring to the next generation of mobile communications, 4G was another rich phrase regularly used by the wireless industry. A loose term for the fourth generation of wireless systems, 4G technologies promised speeds that were about ten times faster than they were on 3G networks. And like its 3G predecessor, the industry gurus started calling it a game-changer the sooner 4G made its name on the wireless paraphernalia. But a closer look at this generation game revealed that the labels like 2G, 3G, and 4G didn't really matter much. Advances were being made and would continue to be made, providing consumers with better, faster mobile broadband, whatever generation it was, and that's what mattered.

There were distinctions, however. One of the key ways in which 4G differed technologically from 3G was in its elimination of circuit switching technology which was common in traditional telecom settings—instead employing an all-IP network. The crucial significance of 4G was lying in the fact that it aimed to be a full-fledged wireless IP network and that it would potentially close the capability gap between wired and wireless worlds. Earlier, the International Telecommunications Union (ITU) had standardized 3G networks for use on both circuit- and packet-based networks, meaning the data would be transferred both through telecom- and Internet-based networks. Conversely, 4G—being the first generation of wireless network technology which was completely IP-based—was set up to use the packet technology only.

The general idea behind 4G was to provide a comprehensive and secure all-IP based solution which, in turn, would facilitate IP telephony, ultra-broadband Internet access, gaming services and streamed multimedia to mobile users. With an all-IP makeup, 4G would allow a treatment of voice calls just like any other type of streaming audio media, thus providing a key turning point for smartphones, which were now increasingly comparable to personal computers. However, while video chat and media consumption were seen to be two key-use cases on the upcoming smart devices, streaming a single video from the web to a mobile device took as much bandwidth as ten phone calls. The 4G services claimed to be capable of download speeds in excess of 5 Mbit/s compared with 3G's real-world maximum of around 1.4 Mbit/s.

The generational change had arrived just in time or so said the marketers. They had grown ever bolder on the heels of the second coming of 3G and the meteoric rise of smartphones. The marketers, who didn't see any trouble in establishing credibility this time around, would declare any new network rollout to be 4G. Take the example of T-Mobile, which rebranded its HSPA+ network as 4G, though the rivals claimed that it was a 3G system that had evolved into 3.5G network over the years. Thanks to bold marketing campaign from T-Mobile, HSPA+, an enhanced version of a 3G technology, became the third flavor of 4G along with front-runners LTE and WiMAX. The marketers also frequently quoted Verizon who had been keen to get its 4G network in place before concluding any agreement with Apple to start selling the iPhone.

Once again, like the early go-go days of 3G, marketing departments had started pushing out the concept of 4G networks years before the engineers even decided what a 4G network was. And when the engineers finally got together to determine what constituted a 4G network under the ITU umbrella in October 2009, they were about two years behind the market trajectory. The ITU set the main criteria that required speed boosts, but more importantly, 4G was required to make more efficient use of the spectrum. The standard body also required that telecom equipment makers provide features that would help guarantee the quality-of-service on wireless networks. True 4G called for peak speeds of 100 Mbit/s for mobile applications such as driving a car down the road and 1 Gbit/s for fixed networks. It was evident that it would take four or five years before the wireless industry started rolling out anything like the ITU's version of 4G.

Much like the transition from 2G to 3G systems, several technologies were developed to provide performance boosts until a proper 4G network was christened. Just as was the case in the 3G saga, marked by the GSM versus CDMA split, 4G technologies were initially separated into two broad camps: LTE and WiMAX. Both technologies were designed to move data rather than voice and offered data speeds of up to 10 Mbit/s. WiMAX hit the technology market a little earlier than LTE and charged a bit less. In the United States, Sprint initially threw its weight behind WiMAX, while AT&T and Verizon chose LTE. There had been quite a bit of debate on whether LTE and WiMAX met all the technical requirements to be classified as 4G technologies.

On the heels of this confusing picture, in 2010, T-Mobile announced plans to upgrade its HSPA network and decided to start branding its HSPA+ upgrade as 4G. HSPA+ was a 21 Mbit/s variant which could generally be added through a software update. Both HSPA 7.2 and HSPA+ had legs over WiMAX in terms of speed; there were many markets where T-Mobile's 21 Mbit/s HSPA+ network was faster than Sprint's WiMAX network.

T-Mobile's move once more sparked the fundamental rethinking of what "4G" really stood for. The term 4G had been used to span from HSPA+ all the way to LTE Advanced, and everything in between, which inevitably added to a lot of confusion. However, the wireless industry at large considered HSPA+ a short term solution at best. Motorola, for instance, pegged 21 Mbit/s HSPA or HSPA+ as a "3.5G" flavor.

While 4G had a valid technical definition, in practice, it had devolved into an essentially empty marketing term. Mobile phone operators in the United States had played fast and loose with the term to try and get an edge over rivals. They were increasingly using '4G' as a marketing terminology to differentiate their networks. The four large U.S. wireless operators seemed to have successfully stolen the 4G show from the ITU. The Geneva, Switzerland–based international telecom standards body was broadly seen as having backed down, saying that the term 4G "might also be applied to the forerunners of the two main technologies: LTE and WiMAX."

ONE NETWORK AT A TIME

On August 8, 2006, then-Sprint CEO Gary Forsee announced that his company would adopt a little known technology called Mobile WiMAX for its fourth-generation mobile data network. Sprint's plans instantly sparked interest because WiMAX wasn't part of the generational shift in cellular technology, but was based on a new model for wireless operators to sell mobile data services. Sprint's chief technology officer Barry West became WiMAX's lead evangelist, promoting it as a pure mobile IP network that followed the model of an Internet service provider (ISP). WiMAX's big backers came from data-centric computer industry—Intel and Google—not from tele-com, and they wanted the future mobile Internet to be built on Internet principles, not on the mobile telecoms model. Meanwhile, a wireless ISP owned by the mobile industry pioneer Craig McCaw was getting similar ideas about the potential of WiMAX technology.

Clearwire, who originally used fixed wireless technologies to deliver residential broadband service in smaller cities across the United States, saw a way to transform itself from a fixed wireless ISP into a mobile broadband carrier. In fact, the Mobile WiMAX standard was evolution of the original fixed-wireless WiMAX specification and aimed to fulfill the criteria of 1 Gbit/s for stationary reception and 100 Mbit/s for mobile reception. Clearwire also happened to have built up a huge collection of radio licenses in the same 2.5 GHz band over which Sprint was planning to deploy its WiMAX network. So it was only a matter of time before Clearwire and Sprint got together. However, the two companies took two years to negotiate a merger pact for a large-scale WiMAX deployment.

In May of 2008, the two companies negotiated a deal that combined their WiMAX operations under the Clearwire umbrella and brought in a US$3.2 billion investment from Intel, Google and several cable companies. In 2010, when Sprint pushed the rollout of its WiMAX network in the United States, the wireless operator named it "4G" to appeal consumers who were now comfortable with 3G lingua franca. The higher speeds of 4G coupled with Sprint's aggressive pricing began to expose consumers to connectivity that was similar to what they've had at home, but in this case, it always lived inside their mobile devices. The world's first commercial mobile WiMAX service, however, was launched by Korea Telecom in Seoul on June 30, 2006.

The crucial benefit that WiMAX had was time-to-market. It was well ahead of the competing 4G technology in development: LTE. WiMAX, a sort of faster and longer-range version of Wi-Fi, was available by the end of 2000s, whereas LTE was expected to take a while to reach its full potential. WiMAX also gave the world the first 4G smartphone—the HTC Evo—a gorgeous device with a 4.3-inch touchscreen which ran Google's Android operating system and featured two cameras, GPS navigation, HDMI output, and mobile hotspot capability. The phone cost US$200 with a two-year contract. Sprint also charged an extra US$10 a month, in addition to its standard data plan, as a service fee to access the 4G network. Ironically, just as Sprint was introducing its 4G network, Apple was unveiling its iPhone 4, which, name aside, ran only on AT&T's 3G network.

Sprint and Clearwire claimed they had years before their competitors could get LTE networks off the ground. They essentially had a four-year head start, but they squandered their time-to-market advantage. Eventually, they ran out of money and four-year head start was whittled down to nine months. Just a few months after the launch of Sprint's WiMAX service, MetroPCS Communications launched the first U.S. LTE network and phone. MetroPCS was also the first U.S. operator to have offered a live Voice over LTE (VoLTE) service and a commercially available VoLTE handset in August 2012. MetroPCS reached an agreement to merge with T-Mobile USA later in October 2012.

LTE was at the standards stage when WiMAX became a commercial reality. Still, LTE was winning the game when it came to mass deployment. As more and more wireless operators embraced LTE, the technology started gaining momentum among handset and infrastructure makers. Two large wireless equipment makers Ericsson and Nokia were not making WiMAX gear. Nokia distanced itself from WiMAX because the technology had no direct links with the existing 3G approach. Sweden's Ericsson, the world's number one telecom-equipment maker, argued that WiMAX was not optimized for voice calls on the move. Even Verizon, a longtime loyalist of Qualcomm and its CDMA technology, started considering LTE, thus joining the camp vying for evolution to the GSM standards path.

If Verizon, the largest wireless service provider in the United States, threw its weight behind LTE, the long reign of Qualcomm's CDMA products could finally come to an end. Indeed, the era of ideological standard wars of the 1990s was over. It was now increasingly apparent that the 4G technology of choice would be LTE and that interest in WiMAX would decline correspondingly. The fact that GSM/wideband-CDMA/LTE was going to be the winning approach had become palpable because of a peculiar development in summer 2010. When Intel acquired the communication business of German chipmaker Infineon Technologies, which had made some good progress on LTE products, it became obvious that WiMAX now was on an uneven footing.

Intel was "WiMAX, WiMAX, WiMAX" at one point. It sank at least US$1.2 billion into supporting WiMAX operators like Clearwire. However, this early backer of WiMAX subsequently shifted gears in favor of LTE, which was clearly gaining favor with the handset makers after winning over wireless operators around the world. Despite the fact that WiMAX came from the data networking world, and it was a crucial merit, LTE's history took it back to the GSM technology and its offshoot GPRS. So it carried a much more effective upgrade path for GSM- and wideband CDMA-focused 3G operators. As a result, with piggyback on existing GSM/3G infrastructure, LTE offered huge benefits of scale which could eventually drive prices down to such a point that WiMAX wouldn't be competitive anymore.

By 2012, Sprint had already started phasing out WiMAX devices and selling its first LTE smartphones in preparation for the network launch in the summer 2013. However, Sprint wasn't going to dump WiMAX entirely; instead it planned to reposition the WiMAX technology as the network for its prepaid customers under the banner of Boost Mobile and Virgin Mobile brands. WiMAX was going to have a niche role to play, predominantly providing DSL replacement services in emerging markets.

THE ANATOMY OF LTE

The concept of the long-term evolution of 3G network based on the European wideband-CDMA technology emerged for the first time during the RAN Evolution Workshop held in Toronto on 2-3 November, 2004. The official name designated for the technology was "3G Long-Term Evolution." The initiative marked the inability of cellular systems to offer high-speed data services, and the quality-of-service (QoS) shortcomings found in Wi-Fi networks, and thus demonstrated the need for a new wireless technology beyond 3G system.

Next, on February 9, 2007, NTT DoCoMo detailed information about trials in which the Japanese mobile operator was able to send data at speeds of up to approximately 5 Gbit/s in the downlink within a 100-MHz bandwidth spectrum to a mobile device moving at 10km/hour.NTT DoCoMo used several technologies, including orthogonal frequency division multiplex (OFDM), multiple input multiple output (MIMO) and maximum likelihood detection. Details of these trials were passed to Third Generation Partnership Project (3GPP) for its consideration.

Long Term Evolution or LTE, as the name suggested, was actually evolution of the existing 3G standard, not a new standard in its own right. While WiMAX emerged from the Wi-Fi world, LTE was a prodigy of the classic GSM technology evolution path. In fact, LTE was long-term evolution of the UMTS technology, and it had built itself on 3GPP technologies like GSM, GPRS, EDGE, W-CDMA, and HSPA. In other words, LTE was simply an advanced form of 3G, also called 3.9G by the ITU. However, LTE represented a paradigm shift from hybrid voice and data networks to data-only networks. The network architecture for LTE was greatly simplified from its predecessors because it was a packet-switched network; it didn't have the capability to handle voice calls and text messages natively.

On December 14, 2009, the first commercial LTE network was deployed in the Scandinavian capitals of Stockholm and Oslo by the Swedish-Finnish network operator TeliaSonera and its Norwegian brand NetCom. TeliaSonera branded the network as 4G. The user terminals and modem devices on offer were manufactured by Samsung, and the network infrastructure was provided by Huawei Technologies in Oslo and Ericsson in Stockholm, respectively. The early LTE handsets started to become available by 2011, and they demonstrated how superb LTE was in transporting video. Still, industry watchers wouldn't expect the widescale deployment of LTE in handsets before 2015. Evolution was the essence here, after all.

The impact of LTE was so big that even powerful carriers from the CDMA camp, like Verizon Wireless and MetroPCS, decided to go with LTE. So what made LTE so special? LTE had brought amazing new capabilities to the cellular business. First, it expanded carrier capacity, meaning more subscribers could be added for a given spectrum assignment. Second, it provided the high data rates needed by the growing number of media-centric applications, mainly video downloads to smartphones and tablets. In other words, LTE networks allowed wireless operators to deliver a lot more data a lot more cheaply. In fact, many consumers found LTE faster than their home broadband connections. Third, it made cellular connectivity more reliable; as a result, LTE would translate to increased engagement and more monetization opportunities. For example, advertisers could serve more ads as mobile users plunged into immersive applications more often and at new locations.

Although it technically didn't comply with all of the 4G specs, mostly in terms of speed, LTE was where most wireless operators seemed to be headed. The technology promised to bring speed boost as well as latency improvements. LTE offered a theoretical capacity of up to 100 Mbit/s in the downlink and 50 Mbit/s in the uplink, and more if MIMO technique for antenna arrays was used. Moreover, the LTE architecture was the first to allow non-hierarchical IP traffic. All the other network schemes specified that all traffic was backhauled to a centralized control point—the switching system—and sent back out, and this could reduce by an order of magnitude the capacity that had to be built into networks. LTE, on the other hand, let traffic route between radio base stations.

LTE required fundamental changes in the base station and handset design due to the higher data rates, wider allowable signal bandwidths, and increasing integration and miniaturization. An LTE network used an evolved node B (eNodeB), essentially an LTE base station, a mobile management entity (MME), a home subscriber server (HSS), a serving gateway (SGW), and a packet data network gateway (PGW). The MME and the HSS handled all duties regarding subscriber access to the network: authentication, roaming rules for subscribers, etc. The SGW essentially acted as a giant router for subscribers, passing data back and forth from the subscriber to the network. The PGW provided the connection to external data networks; the most common data network the PGW provided a connection to was apparently the Internet.

The evolution process of the 3G wireless standard defined the Evolved Universal Terrestrial Radio Access Network (E-UTRAN)-based LTE and System Architecture Evolution (SAE) as the two key building blocks. E-UTRAN handled LTE network's radio part which comprised of base stations termed as eNodeB. There was also evolution of the core network—known as SAE—which was an all-IP network that didn't have separate packet switched data traffic and circuit switched voice traffic. With the exception of the eNodeB, everything was considered as part of the evolved packet core (EPC) network. The eNodeB connected to the EPC at the radio tower level.

OFDM AND MIMO BUILDING BLOCKS

There were two key technologies that enabled LTE to achieve the high data throughput: MIMO and OFDM. LTE used the popular orthogonal frequency division multiplex (OFDM) modulation scheme because it not only provided the essential spectral efficiency to achieve high data rates but also permitted multiple users to share a common channel. OFDM was a form of transmission that used a large number of closely spaced carriers that were modulated with low-rate data. The transmission scheme divided a given channel into many narrower subcarriers. These signals would otherwise be expected to interfere with each other, but by making the signals orthogonal to each another, there was no mutual interference. The data to be transmitted was split across all the subcarriers to give resilience against selective fading from multipath effects.

The OFDM signal in an LTE system comprised a maximum of 2,048 different sub-carriers having spacing of 15 kHz. The actual implementation of the technology was different between the downlink (from the base station to mobile) and the uplink (from mobile to the base station) as a result of the different requirements between the two directions.

A considerable level of experience had been gained in the OFDM technology through its use in Wi-Fi and WiMAX networks. Apparently, OFDM was a modulation format that was very suitable for carrying high data rates, one of the key requirements for LTE. Another primary reason for using OFDM as a modulation format within LTE was its resilience to multipath delays and interference. However, OFDM had some limitations. The subcarriers were closely spaced making OFDM sensitive to frequency errors and phase noise. Furthermore, OFDM was also sensitive to Doppler shift, which could cause interference between the subcarriers.

That's why, for downlink, LTE used orthogonal frequency division multiple access (OFDMA) technology—a variant of OFDM—which allowed subsets of the subcarriers to be allocated dynamically among the different users on the channel. The result was a more robust system with increased capacity. OFDMA was a digital multi-carrier modulation scheme that was widely used in wireless systems but was relatively new to cellular. For the uplink, LTE utilized single-carrier frequency division multiple access (SC-FDMA) scheme for its better peak-to-power average ratio over OFDMA. LTE used the Discrete Fourier Transform spread orthogonal frequency division multiple access (DFTS-OFDMA) scheme for generating an SC-FDMA signal.

Next up, for a radio signal to transmit in both directions, a user device and radio base station must have a duplex scheme. A duplex scheme provides a way of organizing the transmitter and receiver so that they can transmit and receive simultaneously. In the wireless world, there are two forms of duplex operation that are commonly used: frequency division duplex (FDD) and time division duplex (TDD). LTE used both FDD, which employed separate frequencies for downlink and uplink in the form of a band pair, and TDD, which utilized one single range of frequencies in a frequency band, and the band was segmented to support transmit and receive signals in the time domain.

LTE FDD was the more common variant being used in 4G networks. LTE FDD using the paired spectrum was anticipated to form the migration path for the 3G services being used worldwide, most of which used FDD paired spectrum. On the other hand, TDD LTE, also known as TD-LTE, was seen as providing the evolution or upgrade path for the legacy wireless technologies like the Chinese 3G standard TD-SCDMA. The TD-LTE technology had initially been championed principally by China Mobile, which saw TD-LTE as an evolutionary path from the TD-SCDMA technology deployed as a Chinese 3G standard. China Mobile, the largest network operator in the world in terms of the number of subscribers, used TDD frequencies for its 3G network, and it planned to upgrade to the TDD variant of LTE.

However, radio spectrum was a valuable commodity and TD-LTE's use of single frequency rather than paired spectrum was advantageous to mobile operators in countries where spectrum was limited or where an operator only had access to a single unpaired frequency. So TD-LTE had the potential to be much more than a Chinese solution. Moreover, the FDD LTE and TD-LTE versions of the 4G standard were very similar. Mobile devices could support both the FDD and TDD interfaces through a single chipset which meant there wouldn't be any additional cost. That also implied that TDD operations would be able to benefit from the economies of scale that were previously only open to FDD operations.

The other major limitation in communication channels, apart from multipath interference, taken care largely by OFDM technology, was data throughput limitations as a result of Shannon's Law. The multiple-input multiple-output (MIMO) technique provided a way of utilizing the multiple signal paths that existed between a transmitter and receiver to significantly improve the data throughput available on a given channel with its defined bandwidth. MIMO provided LTE with the ability to further improve data throughput and spectral efficiency above that was accomplished through the use of OFDM.

By using multiple antennas at the transmitter and receiver along with some complex digital signal processing, MIMO technology enabled the system to set up multiple data streams on the same channel, thereby increasing the data capacity of the channel. The additional antennas allowed reuse of the same frequency over multiple paths, thus increasing the potential throughput. Here, the transmissions from each antenna must be uniquely identifiable so that each receiver could determine what combination of transmissions had been processed.

The terms "input" and "output" applied to the medium between transmitters and receivers. MIMO radios got more from the bandwidth they occupied than their single-channel equivalents by exploiting differences in the paths between the transmitter and the receiver. If a conventional single-channel radio system created one data "pipe" between the transmitter and the receiver, the object of a MIMO radio system was to create multiple pipes. It did that by creating a mathematical model of multiple paths from transmitters to receivers.

The basic concept of MIMO utilized the multipath signal propagation that was present in most forms of wireless communications. The MIMO scheme, for instance, had been employed in Wi-Fi and WiMAX networks. The technology had been developed over many years. The initial work on MIMO systems focused on basic spatial diversity; the MIMO technology was used to limit the degradation caused by multipath propagation. Up until the 1990s, spatial diversity was often limited to systems that switched between two antennas. Researchers

Arogyaswami Paulraj and Thomas Kailath were first to propose the use of spatial multiplexing using MIMO in 1993 and in the following year they were granted a U.S. patent. However, it was Bell Labs who demonstrated the first laboratory prototype for spatial multiplexing later in 1998.

LTE'S VOICE DILEMMA

The LTE technology had become the new wireless nexus where IT industry leaders from device makers to software developers to network operators were pursuing new business opportunities amid consumers demand for faster and more reliable networks. LTE, for instance, provided second-tier smartphone players like LG Electronics and Nokia—who lagged behind in the heyday of 3G devices—an opportunity to catch up with the likes of Apple and Samsung. Furthermore, the global adoption of LTE as a common 4G standard was also going to heal the rift between the CDMA and GSM camps.

However, unlike previous cellular standards such as GSM and UMTS, LTE didn't have dedicated channels for circuit switched telephony services. And unlike 2G and 3G wireless networks, LTE was going to be a data-only system. So, as a stop-gap measure, 4G wireless operators began handling voice calls by dropping them onto 3G or even 2G networks. This mechanism was called Circuit Switched Fall Back (CSFB). However, when a voice call was initiated by an LTE handset or a call was routed to an LTE handset from a 2G or 3G network, it produced a short but potentially noticeable delay of two to four seconds. This pre-call lag, apart from producing latency, also took a high toll on the device battery. Moreover, having two radios, one for LTE and one for 2G/3G systems, took an enormous toll on phone battery.

Eventually, LTE operators planned to implement Voice over LTE (VoLTE) feature, which was actually Voice over Internet Protocol (VoIP) service offered on the LTE platform, and it would operate simply as a data app on the IP-centric LTE network. VoLTE—formerly known as One Voice—used an extended variant of Session Initiation Protocol (SIP) technology to handle voice calls and text messages. One Voice initiative for VoLTE was launched in February 2010 by a collaboration of over forty companies, including AT&T, Verizon Wireless, Nokia and Alcatel-Lucent.

MetroPCS—later being acquired by T-Mobile—became one of the first mobile operators in the world to deploy VoLTE technology in August 2012. SK Telecom launched a VoLTE service shortly afterward in South Korea. While SK Telecom launched VoLTE service nationally, MetroPCS launched VoLTE only in Dallas, Texas.

The LTE networks of 2013 had limited footprints, forcing phones to continuously check for signals. However, the LTE footprint would gradually expand, and that would ease power constraints. The old GSM and CDMA circuit-switched voice technologies had been optimized over the past two decades to be energy-efficient. So power efficiency in LTE was also bound to improve as both baseband technology and network coverage got better. Eventually, the baseband/modem part in LTE handsets would be optimized for VoIP calling. The power-related issues would also be mitigated over time as components continued to become more power-efficient and LTE handsets didn't need to switch between different modes of voice call processing.

Another crucial issue associated with the VoLTE realization was latency. While throughput measured the bits per second traveling over a network, latency measured how long it took for a request to be answered. The real-time applications like voice, multiplayer games, and video conferencing all suffered when latency was high. The UMTS-based 3G networks had latency of 100 milliseconds to 200 milliseconds for a round trip; 3.5G flavors like HSPA+ took nearly 2 seconds to establish a connection and then as much as 100 milliseconds for the roundtrip thereafter. About 300 milliseconds for a round trip was considered at the limits of acceptability for a VoIP call, but lower latency made the call sound better. Variations on latency within a call could also cause echo and other problems.

The higher the latency the more sluggish services like voice became until they got to a level where users found them unacceptable. Clearly, there was a need for tailoring the network speeds to effectively handle latencies and quality-of-service according to the applications and devices that connected to networks at any given moment. For instance, a video conference call needed extremely low latency and adequate bandwidth to work properly, but a wearable device's upload of healthcare data to the cloud didn't.

The importance of VoLTE as a viable and standardized scheme was crucial because nearly 80 percent of mobile operators' revenues came from voice and SMS traffic as of early 2010s. Mobile operators knew they needed to get VoLTE right because mobile users might not put up with low-quality VoIP conversations which they were otherwise used to get for free over the Internet. The sub-par VoIP experience was fine over the Internet, but mobile users wouldn't stand it while paying up to

US$50 a month. So, unlike streaming services like Skype, VoLTE was going to build quality-of-service feature by guaranteeing a fixed slice of bandwidth for real-time voice services. However, a delay in the launch of VoLTE services could hasten the uptake of third-party VoIP services like Skype, which offered free voice and video services as an Internet app.

Before concluding this section and the chapter, it'd be worth-while to mention that several mobile phone operators had already started offering Wi-Fi calling feature on smartphones in 2013. The voice app, while helping mobile users save money, wouldn't offer the transition from a Wi-Fi call to a cellular call. Some operators, including T-Mobile, had even been charging for these Wi-Fi calls. Nevertheless, services like Wi-Fi calling could provide the wireless industry with the necessary learning curve for handling voice on an entirely new terrain: IP-based data networks.

Ericsson's Mikael Bäckström (left) and TeliaSonera's Erik Hallberg stand next to the network equipment during the launch of the world's first LTE network in Stockholm on December 14, 2009. Ericsson was the network equipment supplier for the LTE launch in Stockholm carried out by TeliaSonera's Swedish subsidiary Telia.

Photo courtesy of Ericsson

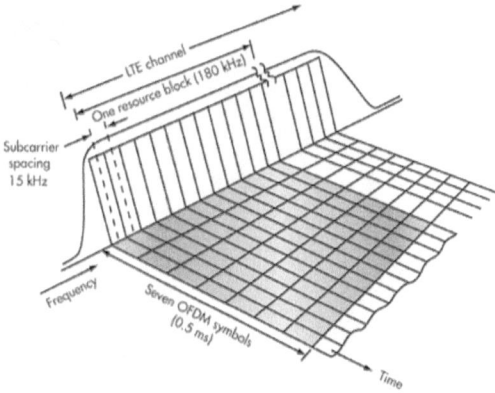

A large number of closely spaced orthogonal sub-carrier signals are used to carry data on several parallel data streams or channels. The OFDM technology, along with MIMO technique, made up the core fabric of the LTE air interface.

Image: *Electronic Design*

6 LTE ON STEROIDS

"I've never found someone who didn't want something faster. But it's not just about speed, the issue of capacity is perhaps more important. These advances allow operators to use more spectrum which means they can handle more subscribers at once."

—Daryl Schoolar, analyst at Ovum

If displays and processors were the main focus for smartphones in 2010, mounting data traffic made 4G the keyword for 2011. The overwhelmed AT&T network had shown the wireless world that smartphones weren't the only value proposition; they also needed faster networks. The demand for wireless data around the globe was expected to double each year from 2014 onward as the population turned to smartphones and similar data-centric devices for instant information anytime, anywhere. By 2015 or so, a predominant majority of phones could have 4G capabilities. However, rather than a sudden revolution, consumers were more likely to go through a gradual transition to the new data technology offering greater speeds.

Meanwhile, the wireless industry was not sitting on its laurels. The next turning point in LTE's exciting journey came on October 21, 2010 when the ITU issued a press release which qualified LTE Advanced (LTE-A) and WiMAX 2 as meeting the requirements for 4G. Consequently,3GPP, the international body that developed the wideband CDMA-based UMTS 3G standard, defined LTE as a 3.9G technology and designated LTE Advanced as the real 4G. LTE Advanced was going to be built on the prior LTE OFDM/MIMO architecture to further increase data rate and subsequently defined in 3GPP Releases 10 and 11.

Inevitably, LTE Advanced was forward and backward compatible with basic LTE, meaning LTE handsets would work on LTE Advanced networks, and LTE Advanced handsets would work on standard LTE networks. That made LTE a stepping stone to the much-higher-capacity LTE Advanced systems. The deployment of LTE Advanced networks was expected in 2014 and beyond.

The LTE Advanced standard promised three times the greater data speeds than basic LTE networks. It boasted five high-octane network features: carrier aggregation, increased MIMO, coordinated multipoint transmission, heterogeneous network (HetNet) support, and relays.

FIVE NOT SO EASY PIECES

The LTE Advanced standard offered considerably higher data rates than the initial releases of LTE. However, while the spectrum usage efficiency had been improved, this alone couldn't provide the required data rates that were being aimed for 4G LTE Advanced. To achieve those very high data rates, it was imperative to increase the transmission bandwidths compared to those networks that could be supported by a single carrier or channel. For a start, 4G operators often found they had a variety of small bands that they had to piece together to provide the required overall bandwidth needed for LTE; making these bands work seamlessly was a key element of the LTE-based heterogeneous network operation.

The method being proposed here was carrier aggregation (CA), also called channel aggregation. Using LTE Advanced carrier aggregation scheme, it was possible to utilize more than one 20 MHz carrier as specified in original LTE specification, and in this way increase the overall transmission bandwidth. Carrier aggregation technique combined up to five 20-MHz channels into one stream to increase data speed, making possible a peak downlink data rate of 1 Gbit/s. It bonded two channels of spectrum even if they happened to reside on entirely different frequency bands.

Carrier aggregation technique enabled the use of fragmented spectrum by dynamically combining blocks of bandwidth to accomplish LTE Advanced data rate of 1 Gbit/s. The end-result was that the network could support much faster connections. Carrier aggregation could double the connection speed of mobile devices, but the tradeoff was that the network would support half the number of users.

Next, while the standard LTE defined MIMO configurations of up to 4x4arrangements, LTE Advanced technology extended that to 8x8 stream with support for multiple transmit antennas in the handset. MIMO was a fundamental element of the LTE system design and the first version of the LTE standard supported 2×2 MIMO in both the downlink and uplink. Subsequent developments extended this capability, and the emerging LTE Advanced systems supported 8×8 MIMO in the downlink and 4×4 MIMO in the uplink.

The potential reception gains from MIMO systems and from beamsteering technique were a function of the number of antennas, and efforts were being made to increase this number for radio systems to up to 8x8 antenna configuration. Beamsteering—the change of direction of a radiation—was accomplished by switching the antenna elements of a radio signal. The use of higher order MIMO and beamsteering in LTE environment, often referred to as coordinated scheduling/coordinated beamforming (CS/CB), was a form of coordination where a mobile device was transmitting to a single transmission or reception point—base station. However, the communication was made with an exchange of radio signals among several coordinated entities.

Third, coordinated multipoint transmission (CoMP)—also known as cooperative MIMO—was a set of techniques using different forms of MIMO and beamforming to send and receive radio signals from multiple cells to a mobile device to reduce interference from other cells and ensure optimum performance at the cell edges. The cell edges in a mobile network were the most challenging; not only the radio signal was lower in strength because of the longer distance from the base station, but also interference levels with the adjacent cells were likely to be higher because the mobile device was closer to them. So providing the same level of service regardless of network technology and areas within the cell could prove to be highly challenging. In order to provide the proper coverage at the cell edges, signal from two or more base stations might be needed.

Coordinated multipoint used coordinated scheduling of transmitters and antennas that weren't collocated to provide greater spatial diversity which could otherwise improve link reliability and data rate. In addition to the increase in the number of antennas, techniques such as beamforming could be used to enable the antenna coverage to be focused where it was needed. The aim was to improve the overall quality for the user as well as improve the utilization of the network.

The biggest merit of coordinated multipoint lied in the fact that it allowed the use of additional frequency bands and enabled effective and efficient use of frequencies. As coordinated multipoint chose the faster one between the two frequency bands for LTE communications, mobile data traffic was optimally distributed to each frequency band, preventing network overload. It was like building an additional road in the always-congested area and then controlling the traffic to ensure smooth flow on both roads.

SK Telecom, which claimed to have launched the world's first commercial LTE Advanced network in summer 2012, actually used an early stage of coordinated multipoint to allow multiple base stations to communicate with a single device simultaneously. SK Telecom launched a pilot service in May 2012 and began full-fledged commercialization on July 1 to ensure a more stable and faster LTE service based on twice wider frequency bandwidth than its competitors. It was also a classical example of how a wireless operator claimed the right to call its network "Advanced" just by adopting a single spec of a lengthy, complex standard.

Fourth, the LTE Advanced standard defined another base station type called relay station. The technologies facilitating high data rates in LTE generally suffered from reduced network capacity at the cell edge where signal levels were lower and interference levels were typically higher. The use of technologies such as MIMO, OFDM, and advanced error correction improved throughput, but they didn't fully mitigate the problems experienced at the cell edge. One of the solutions proposed in LTE Advanced standard was the use of relays. LTE relay was a fixed station that transmitted messages between the base station and mobile device through multihop communication. LTE relays actually received, demodulated and decoded the data and applied error correction to the radio signal and then re-transmitted a new signal with enhanced quality.

LTE relays could also be used to increase the coverage outside the main area and to fill small holes in coverage. Relays didn't need installation of a new base station, so they could be quickly employed to fill in the coverage of a black spot. That way, relays became a cost-effective means of extending LTE coverage to areas where wired backhaul was not viable. LTE relays were easy to install as they required no separate backhaul; moreover, they were small enough to be easily installed at convenient places such as street lamps and walls.

The concept of relaying was not new, but the level of sophistication had continued to grow in the wireless space. The most basic relay method was the use of a radio repeater, which received, amplified and then retransmitted the downlink and uplink signals to overcome areas of poor cellular coverage. Repeaters could improve coverage, but they didn't substantially increase capacity. On the other hand, the aim of LTE relays was to enhance both coverage and capacity. It was not a complete base station but a type of small cell that would fit in the HetNet infrastructure and provide a way to boost data rates and improve the dependability of a wireless link. LTE Advanced 4G standard complemented HetNets—mix of large and small cells—with relay nodes to boost capacity and network flexibility.

Finally, heterogeneous network or HetNet was a multi-layered system of overlapping big and small cells which pumped out cheap bandwidth. The name "heterogeneous" provided a good clue on how a multitude of networks—home and public Wi-Fi, femtocells, picocells, and microcells—come together to form a larger network whole. Several small cells could be distributed within the area covered by a macrocell to provide extra capacity and fill in the gaps in cellular coverage. The concept of the HetNet was a gradual evolution of cellular architecture, not a distinct network unto itself. It arose out of the need for mobile carriers to be able to operate networks consisting of a variety of radio access technologies, formats of cells and many other aspects, and combining them to operate in a seamless fashion.

A HetNet was essentially a combination of small cells and macrocells packaged into a single network. It turned big-tower cellular systems into dense, multi-layered and tremendously high-capacity networks. Mobile phone operators were very excited about moving to a HetNet, which incorporated hundreds if not thousands of small cells or low-powered radio access nodes, which in turn, provided nearly the same functionality for a small region as of a larger radio base station.

However, the HetNet made the network vastly more complex, with the small cells adding thousands more points of interference that needed to be managed. So a new breed of startups was building intelligent software solutions for small cells to make them more manageable within the radio access network (RAN) domain, the crucial part of network spanning from the user device to radio base station. They were, for instance, deploying self-optimizing networks to identify faulty or underutilized cells in real-time and adjust their configuration automatically to provide the optimal level of coverage.

A NEW CELLULAR ARCHITECTURE

One of the enhancements being considered for LTE Advanced was the self organizing network (SON) concept which enabled the efficient use of HetNets. SONs made cellular systems easier to plan, configure, optimize, and manage. With SON, all base stations would be self-configuring, taking into account nearby radio base stations and using internal algorithms to heal, self-optimize, and adapt to nearby stations and other conditions. SONs allowed to flexibly allocating capacity to parts of the cellular network as they were needed by redistributing connections to an optimal configuration at any given time. The idea came about as a result of the need within LTE to be able to deploy many more cells.

In fact, the concept of self-configuring, self-optimizing wireless networks was not a new one. However, in LTE, the ability to automate the management processes emerged as a key technology requirement once the mobile industry moved toward commercialization of 4G systems. The idea behind SONs was to minimize the lifecycle cost of running a network by eliminating manual configuration of wireless infrastructure and dynamically optimizing radio network elements during operation. The LTE standards body 3GPP had created the spec for SON; it was first incorporated into 3GPP Release 8, and further functionality had been progressively added in the following releases of the standard.

Typically, an SON system was a software package with relevant options that were incorporated into an LTE network. The main elements of SON included self configuration, self optimization, and self-healing. The aim for the self configuration aspects of SON was to enable new base stations to become essentially "plug and play" items with as little manual intervention in the configuration process as possible. Self configuration not only helped organize the radio communications aspects, it also configured the LTE network backhaul. Once the LTE system had been set up, self optimization capabilities enabled the base station to optimize the operational characteristics to meet the needs of the overall network. Next, self healing contributed by changing the characteristics of the network to mask the problem until it was fixed. For example, the boundaries of adjacent cells could be increased by changing antenna directions, increasing power levels, etc.

At this point, in the context of a new cellular architecture for 4G wireless, it would be worthwhile to explain the concept of small cell networks. The LTE Advanced system was mostly talked about in relation to five cutting-edge wireless network features profiled in the preceding section. However, if there was a single tech phenomenon that served as the underlying technology for the realization of LTE-based 4G networks, it was the idea of small cell networks.

The first critical juncture in mobile industry's quest for multifold increase in capacity and flexibility of cellular networks came with the realization that the big tower-based macro-umbrella networks that fueled two decades of voice services weren't going to cut it in a data-centric world. So mobile carriers and their infrastructure vendors began designing new types of small cells and base stations intended to deliver intense levels of bandwidth over limited areas. These small cell deployments— pico, micro, metro, femto, etc.—were to evolve into the new heterogeneous network, or HetNet, which would transform cellular systems from coverage- to capacity-focused systems. This implied that the upcoming broadband mobile networks would carry hundreds of thousands if not millions of cells.

LTE became a driving force behind the small-cell movement. In retrospect, mobile operators could have created far more capacity if they deployed smaller cells, reusing the spectrum they had to the nth degree. However, they couldn't build the density of cells necessary to support the demands for mobile data. It was a hard feat to pull off because at any time, when two signals used the same frequency in the same space, there would be interference. So, for several years, the mobile industry had been trying to figure how to mitigate that interference. That's why it took so long to convert an ordinary picocell into a true small cell. Now, instead of cramming picocells onto cellular gaps, mobile operators would mount picocells on lamp posts and buildings, right under the gaze of macro towers with which they would share the airwaves.

At first, small cell network would function much like an extension of the large cell counterparts. The network would pass mobile users from big cell to small cell and vice versa. However, the key difference was that when mobile users occupied the small cell, they would have a lot more bandwidth at their disposal. Mobile devices would be able to link to multiple cells simultaneously, and the same signals that once interfered with one another would reinforce one another creating an even more powerful connection. The high-capacity Wi-Fi networks would also get layered in, creating a heterogeneous network in which mobile devices could establish multiple simultaneous connections using multiple radio technologies. Apparently, that boiled down to an awful lot of bandwidth.

With revenue per bit falling, costs for deployment must be kept to a minimum while ensuring that the network was operating to its greatest efficiency. So femtocells and other microcell schemes were an integral part of the LTE deployment strategy. A femtocell was a small, low-power cellular base station, typically designed for use in a home or small business. Typically, the range of a standard macrocell was up to 35 kilometres or 22 miles; a microcell was less than two kilometers wide; a picocell was 200 meters or less; and a femtocell was on the order of 10 meters.

In 2013, the U.S. mobile carriers were getting ready for their first small cell deployments with an aim of implementing multi-technology heterogeneous networks. The two main deployment scenarios for small cells were in rural areas with poor or no indoor coverage, probably using co-channel deployment, and in dense areas to provide high data rates and capacity. The main goal of these shrunken cells, however, was to put massive amounts of bandwidth precisely where mobile users were using it: shopping malls, public areas, business districts, etc. Networking equipment maker Cisco estimated that Wi-Fi and femtocells would handle nearly half of all mobile traffic by 2017.

Another crucial subject in relation to data-centric 4G cellular architecture was the advent of shared data plans. In early 2010s, 4G networks were partially in place, but the mobile establishment was wrestling with new questions: how and what do they charge for these fancy new 4G services? Mobile phone operators were obviously going through a period of pricing and service experimentation while they tried to work out the business model. It was a 3G redux in a sense that the wireless industry found itself at a similar inflection point where it had built the networks, but it still hadn't worked out the business model.

In summer 2012, Verizon Wireless lifted the curtain on its long-awaited shared-data plans that allowed mobile users to put additional devices under one umbrella. The plans would offer unlimited voice, messaging, and a block of data for a flat cost, plus a fee for each device that would be drawing on that data. Such plans, which encouraged increased data use by making it easier to add devices such as tablets, also increased the operator's grip on paying for data that was once offered on an unlimited basis. Verizon Wireless—a joint venture of Verizon Communications Inc. and Vodafone Plc—would allow users to cover up to ten devices under one contract in its "Share Everything" data plan. A month after Verizon introduced a wireless plan that allowed users to share data across multiple devices, AT&T followed suit.

While European operators were testing the potential of 4G being a premium-priced data service, charging more for a megabyte of LTE than a megabyte of HSPA+, large U.S. operators like AT&T and Verizon were barreling ahead with shared data plans. More business models could emerge as mobile operators started experimenting with enterprise and machine-to-machine data plans. Nevertheless, the so-called data hogs, the nearly 3 percent of smartphone users who ate up 40 percent of the data, were no longer a stigma in the wireless world. Thanks to LTE networks and applications like Netflix, YouTube, online games and Skype, the mainstream smartphone user was also graduating into a high-bandwidth consumer. Five years after the iPhone kicked off a surge in demand for mobile data, the U.S. mobile operators like AT&T and Verizon were learning to love data hogs. The faster the network, the more that people would use it.

WAITING FOR 5G

Voice had long been the primary revenue driver for mobile phone operators. While advancements in tech hotspots like mobile data, mobile Internet and mobile broadband won much of the space in the trade press, voice service remained the primary source wireless carriers' earnings. However, the crossover point between voice and data traffic finally arrived in the year 2013. According to a report from Chetan Sharma Consulting, during the third quarter of 2013, data accounted for 48 percent of all U.S. mobile industry revenues. The LTE-based 4G networks and smartphones were clearly two major factors in this reversal of fortunes.

According to Visiongain, a market research firm, there were an estimated 125 million LTE users in 2012; that was up from a mere 10 million in 2011. Also, by 2012, according to estimates from networking giant Cisco, global mobile data traffic was nearly doubling each year. Not surprisingly, therefore, in just two years after the LTE launch in 2011, Verizon had moved 21.6 million subscribers over to its LTE network. Verizon planned to finish its network build in mid-2013, six months ahead of schedule, offering LTE everywhere it had the 3G network coverage. Verizon had launched its first LTE phone—the HTC Thunderbolt—in March 2011. Here, it would be worthwhile to mention that the leader in LTE adoption was South Korea, which had moved nearly half of its mobile users to the new technology.

Mobile broadband networks accounted for nearly a quarter of the world's mobile cellular connections by early 2013. That came down to 1.6 billion 3G and 4G connections. The wireless industry defined mobile broadband as any 3G or 4G technology that could stream a video signal to a smartphone or tablet with a decent connection. However, 3G subscriptions made up the bulk of this number with LTE and WiMAX networks contributing merely 5 percent of these 1.6 billion subscriptions. In fact, 4G networks represented just 1 percent of the mobile connections across the world in 2013. However, that 1 percent was generating 14 percent of the overall traffic because speed did matter. When 4G reached its anticipated 10 percent adoption rate in 2017, according to Cisco estimates, the technology would drive 45 percent of the total mobile traffic.

It took twelve long years for 3G technologies to touch half of the world's population, but LTE networks were being deployed much faster than their 3G predecessors. By 2017, LTE would cater to nearly 50 percent of the world's mobile data traffic, a remarkable feat considering the first commercial LTE systems went live only in 2010.

In 2013, the state of the 4G technology was rather clear, though it was still a work in progress. New LTE releases were yet to come, and it would take a decade or more for LTE, especially LTE Advanced to dominate cellular coverage. The technology had been true to its name; it would evolve over a longer term. While much had been answered in terms of technical work, a lot had still to be answered. The fact that there was no set finish line to qualify for LTE Advanced networks inevitably meant that some part of that evolving work could overlap with the next-generation wireless network: 5G.

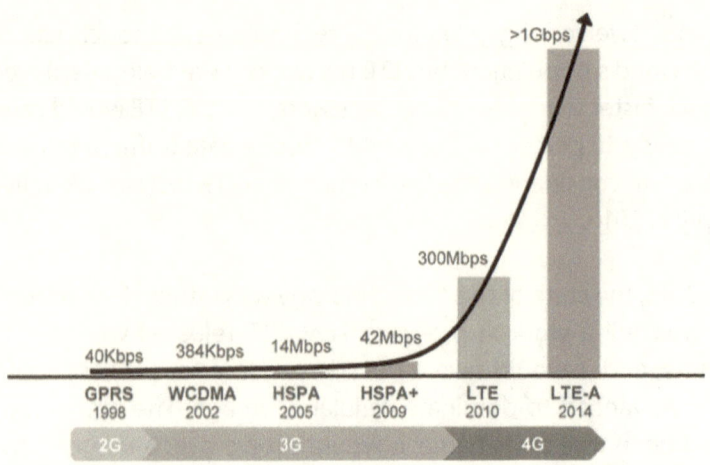

The LTE Advanced standard promised three times greater data speeds than original LTE and comprised of five technology features: carrier aggregation, increased MIMO, coordinated multipoint transmission, heterogeneous network (HetNet) support, and relays.

Image source: Ericsson

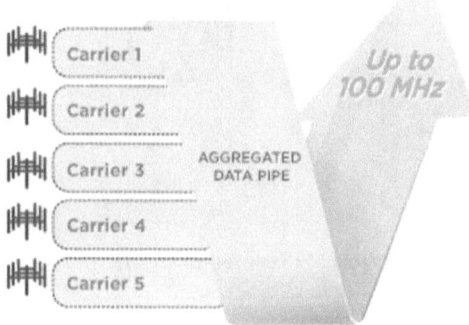

LTE Advanced technology allowed aggregation of up to five carriers, taking combined frequency spectrum to 100 MHz, to provide extremely high peak data rates, theoretically over 1 Gbit/s.

Image courtesy of Qualcomm

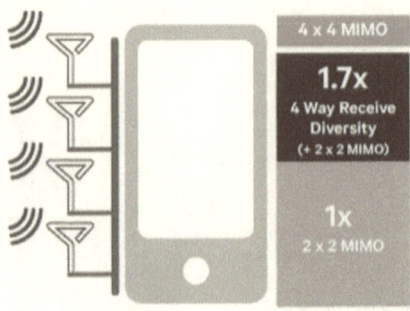

Most gain from 4x receive diversity

Advanced antenna techniques such as higher-order MIMO were an important part of LTE Advanced architecture for substantially increasing data rates for high-bandwidth apps like video streaming. The next logical step from early 2x2 MIMO configuration used in LTE networks was to implement 4×4 MIMO configuration (shown in the above image), and ultimately bring most of the antenna gain through 8x8 MIMO configuration.

Image credit: Qualcomm

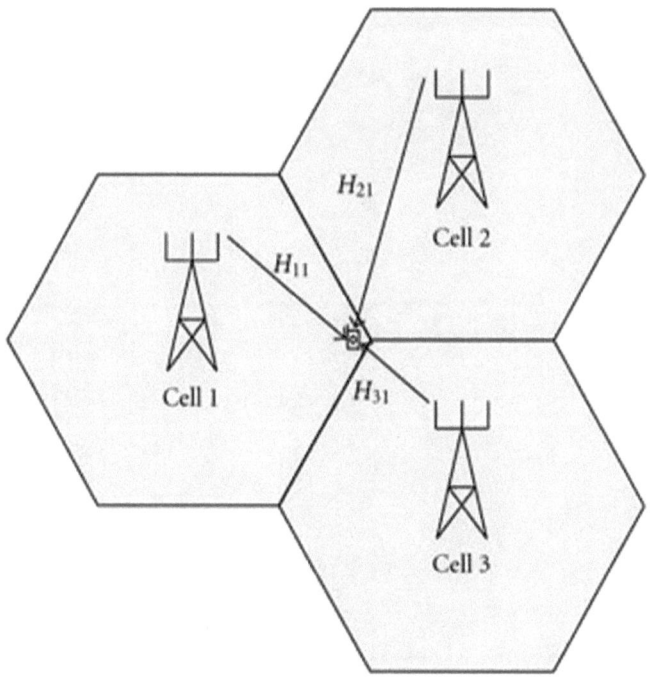

The CoMP technology was made up of a range of different techniques that enabled the dynamic coordination of transmission and reception over a variety of base stations. The main objective of CoMP was to improve network performance at cell edges. It essentially turned the inter-cell interference (ICI) into useful signal, especially at the cell borders where performance might be degraded.

Image source: www.3g.co.uk

7 THE VISION OF 5G

"The world is going increasingly wireless. This is going to be a very good business for a very long time."

— Howard Ward, chief investment officer at Gamco Asset Management

There were several keys to the fulfillment of the mobile Internet paragon: the evolution of user terminals being the prime one. The next biggest barrier was speed. Sending data to and from mobile devices was initially a tedious process. Speed peaked at around 14.4 Kbit/s, a rate that didn't allow much beyond transmitting e-mails and checking websites for small amounts of information. A lot was at stake for faster wireless data networks. For instance, the future of mobile commerce was intertwined with the realization of fatter network pipes. Mobile commerce could become a substantial source of revenue for wireless companies once speedier networks were built out. The capabilities of 3G and 4G technologies would also make applications such as messaging and web browsing more appealing to users and enable new ones such as music downloads, streaming audio and video, and mobile gaming. Although these activities would chiefly be used for non-commerce applications, they would give mobile commerce a boost, nonetheless.

Wireless operators were not fighting to become dumb pipes after all. But the flip side for the network carriers like AT&T was that they had a lot more at stake than did the newcomers like Apple and Google. For instance, the more iPhones were sold, the more unhappy users could be because of the network congestion. The iPhone had created the consumerization of mobile data services, but on platforms like the mobile Internet, consumerization was generally accompanied by a catastrophic decline in per bit revenue for the mobile service provider. The world had witnessed how Apple's iPhone crippled swaths of AT&T's wireless network as users complained about dropped calls and network delays. The network that pioneered the smartphone in collaboration with the iPhone also topped in consumer dissatisfaction.

The post-iPhone smartphone enterprise had brought down the traditional "one-size-fits-all" pricing model that originally made the mobile Internet more affordable to a greater number of people. Consumers naturally preferred unlimited plans, but mobile carriers couldn't provide them due to limited infrastructure, so they dropped unlimited plans in favor of tiered data buckets. Mobile data was a finite resource, so mobile phone carriers, responding to the bandwidth challenge, chose not to treat data like a commodity. They carved off 5 percent of their heaviest users and stigmatized them.

Fast forward to 2014: the 4G wireless engine was now unleashing a new era of innovative business models in which giant mobile carriers were operating in a true spirit of upstarts. After Verizon's shared-data plan, in early 2014, T-Mobile announced it would pay mobile users who were willing to dump AT&T, Verizon, or Sprint for its service. The "Operation UnCarrier" would pay up to US$300 for their old devices; T-Mobile would also pay off mobile users' final bills and early termination fees from their previous carriers, up to US$350 per line. Then, during the 2014 CES, AT&T threw another stunner when it announced the "Sponsored Data" plan which would allow brands to subsidize mobile data so that streaming content wouldn't cut into mobile users' monthly data allotments. AT&T claimed this could set up a tiered mobile Internet in which enterprises could pay for their employees' work-related data consumption or advertisers could show their ads without eating up consumers' data plans.

How consumers would respond to these mobile data packages was going to define the course of action for wireless operators, but one thing was certain: the relentless march of bandwidth had started with the ascent of smartphones, and it would only go farther. People had started streaming movies from the web to their smartphones and iPads, and as they did so, the demand for mobile bandwidth grew faster than anyone ever imagined. So it became imperative that mobile phone operators figured out how to slice and dice data into an appealing tiered plan because once 4G network deployments passed halfway mark, there would be no looking back. Wireless operators were going to become mobile ISPs with voice businesses on the side.

MOBILE INTERNET OF THINGS

While mobile carriers continued to tinker with consumer data pricing, they had also started to think beyond smartphones and focus on the Internet of Things, connecting everything from tablets to cars to home appliances. AT&T and General Motors, for instance, planned to embed LTE technology into millions of cars as an upgrade to GM's OnStar infotainment service. Likewise, some mobile operators were demonstrating connected home and connected city applications, sticking LTE radios in smart utility meters and public transit and healthcare devices. In fact, the whole idea behind the fifth generation wireless (5G) was to build ubiquitous networks offering plentiful and cheap mobile data and create a more efficient life for people.

Mobile phone operators had long dreaded of becoming the dumb pipes of raw bandwidth. The Internet of mobile things was their opportunity to seize the moment and manage connections and services in the new wireless order. AT&T had already taken full control over its wireless business back in 2006, and now it aspired to facilitate digital life for its customers through ideas like connected home and connected car. Next up, Verizon Communications paid US$130 billion for Vodafone's 45 percent stake in Verizon Wireless to take complete control of its mobile business and run both wireline and wireless businesses under the same roof. The deal would dissolve the venture the two companies formed in April 2000, which was one of the initial partnerships for the newly launched Verizon, created as a result of the merger of Bell Atlantic and GTE.

In 2013, the future growth of the wireless industry seemed to be associated with the "Internet of Things" hooked up to cars, wearable appliances and household objects. Some of these things would connect to wired home networks, some of them would be linked to mobile networks, and some of them would need to connect to both. Verizon was among the companies who believed in this brave new world of connected cars, kitchen appliances and wearable gizmos, and was likely trying to lay grounds for this new business through a greater synergy between its wired and wireless networks.

Coming back to 5G wireless systems, the fundamental concept of 5G demanded the network to be not a monolithic entity. One of the key merits of the futuristic 5G networks was going to be their ability to handle billions of connected devices and myriad of traffic types. In other words, what was transformative about the 5G technology was its ability to offer different capabilities for different traffic types: it could serve industrial Internet and Facebook applications at the same time. That's why the key elements of these futuristic networks spanned from smart antennas to ultra-dense deployments and from improved coordination between base stations to device-to-device communication.

In the 1990s, the concept of remotely monitoring and controlling distributed assets and devices was mostly reserved for large and expensive investments like power plants and dams. Fast forward to 2013, connected products were expanding to e-books, cars, power monitoring and smart grid, manufacturing, fast food, security, healthcare, and more. LTE offered the promise of transforming vehicles and other entities into real mobile communications centers, providing heightened security, infotainment and a host of outbound data flow. By 2020, billions of things, from clothes to cars and from body sensors to tracking tags, were forecast to be connected to mobile networks. That could consume 1,000 times as much data as mobile gadgets of early 2010s, so while mobile operators rushed to roll out 4G networks, the wireless establishment was already beginning to define 5G wireless standards.

Mark Weiser's work on "ubiquitous computing" at Xerox PARC back in 1988 had conceived wireless data as the underlying technology for a computing environment that enabled personal mobility of computer users. Now some people in the wireless industry believed that the next generation of wireless networks—5G—could embody that vision of "ubiquitous computing" by offering mobile users the ability to access the applications from any platform, anywhere, any time. To create such an environment, the industry needed to integrate various applications working in harmony with intelligent sensor networks. For instance, users' car sent SMS to their mobile phones if someone tried to open the door while they were away from their cars. Or a user's home security camera was hooked to the Internet, so that he or she could view the living room on his or her mobile phone screen.

THE 2020 NETWORK

The 4G-centric small cell networks would bring wireless industry an alternate yet complimentary high-capacity system. In the meantime, work continued toward the next big thing, more specifically the fifth generation (5G) of cellular networks. In 2013, 4G was still in its infancy, and 5G was a mere concept. Fifth-generation wireless was a term referred to research papers and projects for the next major phase of mobile telecommunications standard beyond the4Gplatforms. It was very likely that 5G would simply stay on the same path as 4G and LTE, using higher frequencies and wider bandwidths to achieve even higher data rates.

However, while 4G was still evolving, and 5G was in an embryonic stage, the question was "what's the big rush?" First and foremost, mobile data traffic was growing exponentially. Moreover, until now, the wireless industry had mostly focused on raw bandwidth. However, the 5G networking debate was eventually moving beyond the tired discussion of raw speed and was starting to focus on pervasive connectivity to lay grounds for a fast and resilient link to the Internet whether a mobile user was in a subway train, at the top of a skyscraper, or in an exhibition center.

According to a 2011 study from Morgan Stanley, the growth curve for the mobile Internet could be around twelve times as steep as for the desktop Internet, which we remember how transformative that was during the 1990s. The report called the speed of the mobile Internet take-up a revolution the likes of which people haven't seen before. Mobile phones were reaching into the furthest corners of the world, and according to an ITU study, at the end of 2011, there were as many mobile phones as people inhibiting the planet: nearly 6 billion. Though most of these handsets were feature phones with limited capabilities, during this decade, the technologies would become so cheap that virtually every phone sold would become what the industry called a smartphone in 2013.

And every one of these phones would be constantly connected to the Internet. So what would happen when most of the inhabitants of this planet carried a gadget that gave them instant access to pretty much all of the world's information? The implications for almost every aspect of life were dizzying. The good news was that the basic vision of the mobile Internet was in place by the year 2013. With a steady rise in network speed, it was hoped that the dream of a pervasive wireless network would turn into a reality with smartphones making mobile data services as easy to use as the ubiquitous telephone system.

Enter 5G networks. For a start, on November 1, 2012, the Mobile and wireless communication Enablers for the Twenty-twenty Information Society (METIS) was formed as a consortium of technology companies and universities to identify the most promising 5G solutions by early 2015.The consortium could take the notion of small cell networks to a whole new level to create super-dense networks, which could put tiny cells as pervasively as in every room. Though the big wireless operators and vendors like NTT DoCoMo, Orange, Alcatel-Lucent, and Ericsson were all part of METIS, the consortium went beyond the traditional wireless industry norms to include carmakers such as BMW to explore areas like vehicle-to-vehicle communication.

In 2013, the European Commission (EC) committed 50 million euros for research to deliver 5G mobile technology by 2020.The overall technical goal was to provide a system concept that supported 1,000-times higher mobile system spectral efficiency as compared with LTE deployments. Europe's flagship 5G project METIS was considering a variety of technologies, including new data coding and modulation techniques, better interference management, densely-layered small cells, multihop networks, and advanced receiver designs. A key characteristic of 5G networks would be the use of many diverse systems that must work together. Millimeter-wave technology was also a part of that bigger pie.

Next up, in 2013, the European Telecommunications Standards Institute (ETSI), which had set up the 3GPP venture back in 1998 to create 3G specifications based on the evolution of GSM technologies, kick-started the 5G Public Private Partnership (5GPPP) project to facilitate a blueprint for the deployment of 5G in the years after 2020. The EC would spend 700 million euros over the next seven years to bankroll the effort through 5GPPP and help researchers create a working 5G technology. Similar efforts to ramp up 5G collaborative research were underway in China, Japan and South Korea, albeit at a much lower scale.

MILLIMETER WAVES FOR 5G

In summer 2013, Samsung generated some media buzz when it announced a new beamforming antenna that could send and receive mobile data faster than 1 Gbit/s data rates over a distance of 2 kilometers. Samsung's Advanced Communications Lab in Suwon, South Korea demonstrated a prototype transmitter that was able to send data at speeds of more than 1 Gbit/s to two receivers moving up to 8 kilometers per hour. Using transmission power no higher than used in 4G base stations, the communication devices were able to connect to up to 2 km away when in line of sight of each another. For non-line-of-sight connections, the range shrank to about 200 to 300 meters. The prototype was a matchbook-size array of 64 antenna elements equipped with custom-built signal-processing systems.

By dynamically varying the signal phase at each antenna, the transmitter-receiver combo or transceiver generated a beam just 10 degrees wide that it could switch rapidly in any direction as if it were a hyperactive searchlight. To connect with one another, a base station and mobile radio would continually sweep their beams to search for the strongest connection, getting around obstructions by taking advantage of reflections. The transmitter and receiver worked together to find the best beam path. Although the prototype was designed to work at 28 GHz frequency, Samsung engineers claimed the system could be applied to most frequencies between about 3 and 300 GHz.

Cellular networks had always occupied frequencies lower on the spectrum, where carrier waves tens of centimeters long—hundreds of megahertz—passed easily around obstacles and through the air. However, this coveted spectrum was now heavily used, making it difficult for mobile phone operators to acquire more of it. At the same time, 4G networks had just about reached the theoretical limit on how much data they could squeeze into a given amount of spectrum. So, wireless engineers began looking toward higher frequencies, where radio use was lighter. Here, regulators could free as much as 100 GHz of millimeter-wave spectrum for mobile communications—about 200 times what mobile networks used in 2013. Wireless systems that used millimeter waves already existed for fixed, line-of-sight transmissions.

For instance, the upcoming indoor wireless standard known as WiGig would allow multi-gigabit data transfers between devices in the same room. WiGig was an extremely high-speed, but short-range wireless LAN technology that promised to link ultra-high-performance broadband appliances and peripherals with up to 6 Gbit/s connections. The technology behind WiGig was fairly different from Wi-Fi in terms of the performance, range and use cases, and it didn't interoperate with traditional Wi-Fi networks. Moreover, advanced millimeter wave systems were functioning in short-range personal-area networks (PANs) for home video transfer, automotive radar, and cellular/hotspot backhaul.

However, there were reasons for the wireless industry to have long avoided millimeter waves for broader mobile coverage. For a start, millimeter waves didn't penetrate solid materials very well. Next, these waves had a tendency of losing more energy than lower frequencies over long distances because they were readily absorbed or scattered by gases, rain, and foliage. Moreover, because a single millimeter-wave antenna had a small aperture, it needed more power to send and receive data than was practical for cellular systems. The wireless industry was try-ing to overcome these challenges by using an array of multiple antennas to concentrate radio energy in a narrow, directional beam, thereby increasing gain without upping transmission power. Such beamforming arrays long used for radar and space communications could now be used in next-generation cellular systems.

So, on the outset, millimeter-wave technology didn't seem to make useful replacement for cellular systems, where base sta-tions encompassed more than a kilometer of distance. However, in the coming years, as described in the preceding section, many base stations would likely be much smaller. Therefore, not only could millimeter-wave technology merit for those small cells, it could also provide a simple, inexpensive alternative to backhaul links, which connected cellular base stations to mobile operators' core networks. The small cells would be mounted on street poles, building walls and every form of urban fixture where access to cable or fiber wasn't readily available, and the cost of laying fiber was prohibitive. LTE required fat backhaul pipes and millimeter wave technologies could provide both the reach and capacity at the right prices for the HetNet backhaul.

Millimeter wave transmission systems suited to small cell backhaul for two reasons. First, it was relatively easy to get licenses for big blocks of millimeter wave spectrum, which would allow mobile operators to deploy large backhaul pipes of over 1 Gbit/s. While a single small cell might not need that much capacity, the complexity of HetNets would require daisy-chaining many small cells together, each cell passing its load down the line. The final backhaul link in such a mesh or chain could end up handling dozens of cells worth of traffic before it dumped the data onto a core fiber network. Second, by definition, the HetNet would be composed of densely packed cells in urban environments, meaning millimeter wave wouldn't have to travel far between hops.

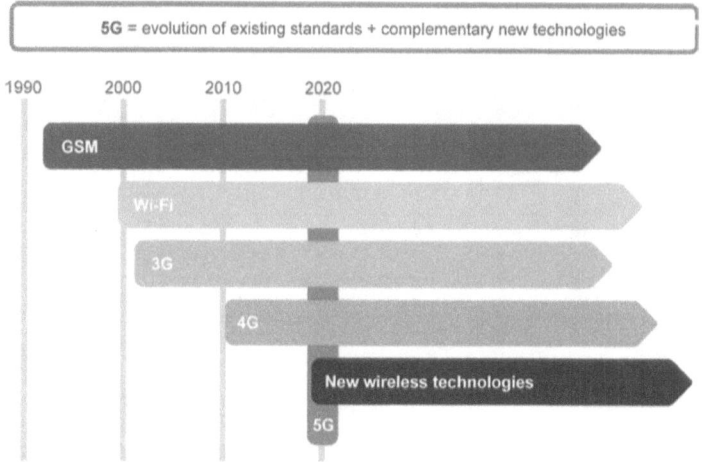

The 5G technology recipe was made up of evolution of existing standards and a range of complementary new technologies, including cloud computing, Internet of Things and millimeter wave communications.

Image: Ericsson

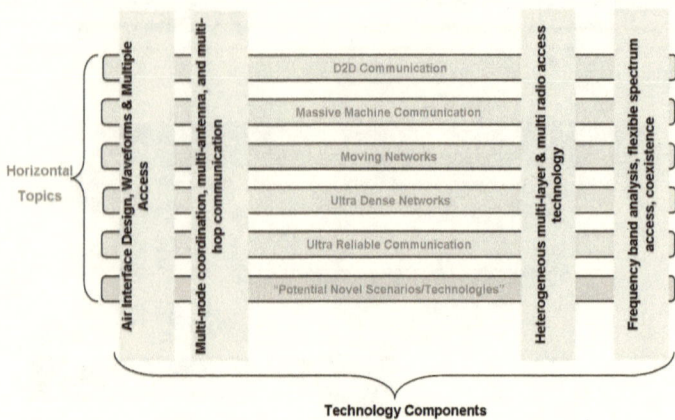

Technology Components

METIS stood for Mobile and wireless communications Enablers for the Twenty-twenty Information Society. The main objective of this European project was to lay the foundation of 5G, the next generation mobile and wireless communications system.

Image courtesy of METIS

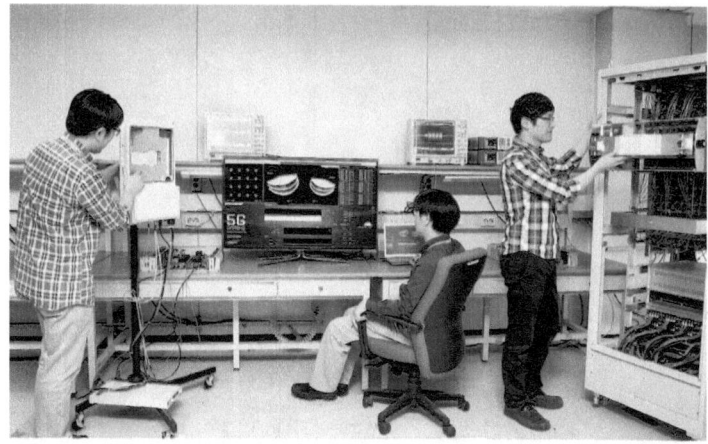

In summer 2013, Samsung demonstrated a transmitter prototype with beamforming antenna, which sent data at a speed of 1 Gbit/s to two receivers that were 2 kilometers away and were moving at the speed of 8 kilometers per hour. Engineers Wong-Suk Choi (left), Daer-Yong Lee (middle) and Byungh-Wan Lee are seen here testing millimeter wave equipment at Samsung's Advanced Communications Lab in Suwon, South Korea.

Photo: Samsung Electronics

Ted Rappaport, the founding director of NYU Wireless at the Polytechnic Institute of NYU, carried out some pioneering efforts on the directional beaming antenna technology. The work at his lab focused on the physical properties of millimeter wave communications.

Photo: New York University

NOTES

Prologue

Brendan Greeley, "Overstating Smartphone Data Hogs?" *Bloomberg Businessweek*, February 9, 2011.

David Ayala, "Dreaming Up the Smartphone of the Future," *GeekTech*, February 18, 2010.

Dulan McGrath, "AT&T adopts tiered pricing for smartphone data access," *EE Times*, June 2, 2010.

Jolie O'Dell, "What Makes a Smartphone a Superphone?" *Mashable*, July 12, 2010.

JP Mangalindan, "Unlimited data, R.I.P.," *Fortune*, June 4, 2010.

Kevin C. Tofel, "Flat-Rate Data Plans Are Dead. Is That a Good Thing?" *Gigaom*, November 4, 2010.

Thomas Claburn, "Is a closed iPhone doomed to fail?" *InformationWeek*, January 11, 2007.

Chapter 1

Apostolis K. Salkintzis and ChristodoulosChamzas, "An Insight into MOBITEX Architecture," *IEEE Persoanl Communications*, February 1997.

ArikHesseldahl, "Wireless PDAs Circa 2007," *Forbes*, April 25, 2002.

Cliff Edwards, "No Cartwheels for Handspring," *Bloomberg Businessweek*, April 2, 2001.

"PDA to Smartphone Evolution," *Techsplosive*, February 11, 2009.

Richard Ernsberger Jr., "Electronic Mail on the Airwaves," *Newsweek*, April 5, 1993.

Chapter 2

David Pringle, "Don't Expect Cure For All Wireless Ills From GPRS Phone," *The Wall Street Journal*, June 15, 2001.

"GPRS as the gateway to 3G," Northstream AB press release, February 20, 2002.

Kendra Wall, "Splitting the spectrum," *Upside*, August 31, 2001.

"Pass the painkillers," *The Economist*, May 3, 2001.

Stephen H. Wildstrom, "Wireless Data: Call Back Later," *Bloomberg Businessweek*, March 4, 2002.

Stuart Corner, "Wireless networks struggling to cope with smartphone & data boom," *iTWire*, August 3, 2009.

Chapter 3

Craig Matsumoto, "Panel decries lethargy in 3G," *EE Times*, June 11, 2001.

Dan Briody, "3G is no laughing matter," *Red Herring*, February 27, 2001.

Dan Devine, "Wireless data network dominance behind AT&T, Verizon smartphone wars," *TechTarget*, October 22, 2009.

Lucas van Grinsven, "Motorola sees no European 3G adoption before 2004," *Reuters*, October 25, 2001.

Chapter 4

Ben Charny, "Wi-Fi phones make a splash," *CNET News*, August 5, 2004.

Bob Goodman, "The technologies that will save us from the "mobile data crunch"" *Gigaom*, March 10, 2013.

Jared Headley, "Wi-Fi offers huge opportunities, but here's how companies could blow it," *Gigaom*, March 9, 2013.

Kevin Fitchard, "The next generation of Wi-Fi hotspots is coming," *Gigaom*, February 23, 2012.

Kevin Fitchard, "We already use Wi-Fi more than cellular; Why not continue the trend?" *Gigaom*, July 10, 2012.

Chapter 5

Christopher Ryan, "The Next iPhone: Are We Ready for 4G?" *Gigaom*, March 22, 2010.

Craig Mathias, "Getting early handle on 4G," *EE Times*, November 12, 2001.

Dan Jones, "Cisco: 4G Eats 14 Percent of World's Mobile Data," *Light Reading*, February 5, 2013.

"Generational change," *The Economist*, December 3, 2010.

Glenn Fleishman, "The state of 4G: it's all about congestion, not speed," *Ars Technica*, March 29, 2010.

Kevin Fitchard, "A brief history of Sprint's on-again, off-again affair with Clearwire," *Gigaom*, December 17, 2010.

Kevin Fitchard, "Voice calls over 4G LTE networks are battery killers," *Gigaom*, November 29, 2010.

Lou Frenzel, "The Evolution Of LTE," *Electronic Design*, January 8, 2013.

"LTE, WiMAX and the end of history," Matt Hatton's blog, June 15, 2009.

PriyaGanapati, "Everything You Need to Know About 4G Wireless," *Wired*, June 4, 2010.

Stacey Higginbotham, "Will the Real 4G Please Stand Up?" *Gigaom*, November 4, 2010.

Tony Daltorio, "Long Term Evolution vs. WiMax: The 4G Technology Showdown," *Investment U Research*, August 23, 2010.

"Verizon: Long Term Evolution of 4G and the Internet," *C114*, July 27, 2010.

Chapter 6

Ian Poole, "4G LTE Advanced Tutorial," *Radio-Electronics.com*.

StamatisGeorgoulis, "LTE to LTE-Advanced: What You Need to Know Right Now," *EE Catalog*, September 27, 2013.

Chapter 7

Ariel Bleicher, "Millimeter Waves May Be the Future of 5G Phones," *IEEE Spectrum*, June 13, 2013.

Kevin Fitchard, "Can millimeter waves solve the small cell backhaul problem," *Gigaom*, April 11, 2012.

Kevin Fitchard, "Ericsson CEO: We've got 4G networks. Now what do we do with them?" *Gigaom*, February 27, 2013.

Kevin Fitchard, "Ericsson: The summertime forecast calls for small cells & more mobile bandwidth," *Gigaom*, January 31, 2013.

Kevin Fitchard, "What's in a 'G'? Why terms like 5G and LTE-Advanced are important," *Gigaom*, June 28, 2013.

INDEX

ABOUT THE AUTHOR

Majeed Ahmad is former Editor-in-Chief of *EE Times Asia*, a sister publication of *EE Times*. While being the Editor-in-Chief at Global Sources, a Hong Kong–based publishing house, he also spearheaded magazines relating to electronic components, consumer electronics, and computer, security and telecom products.

This is his fifth book on wireless and smartphones. His first four book titles are *Smartphone*, *Nokia's Smartphone Problem*, *Mobile Commerce 2.0.*, and *Essential 4G Guide*.

He is currently associated with a number of technology publications as a contributing writer and Editor-at-Large. He has been a technology and trade journalist for more than 18 years.

www.ingramcontent.com/pod-product-compliance
Lightning Source LLC
Chambersburg PA
CBHW021428170526
45164CB00001B/151